Questioning Extreme
Programming

The XP Series

Kent Beck, Series Advisor

Extreme Programming, familiarly known as XP, is a discipline of business and software development that focuses both parties on common, reachable goals. XP teams produce quality software at a sustainable pace. The practices that make up "book" XP are chosen for their dependence on human creativity and acceptance of human frailty.

Although XP is often presented as a list of practices, XP is not a finish line. You don't get better and better grades at doing XP until you finally receive the coveted gold star. XP is a starting line. It asks the question, "How little can we do and still build great software?"

The beginning of the answer is that, if we want to leave software development uncluttered, we must be prepared to completely embrace the few practices we adopt. Half measures leave problems unsolved to be addressed by further half measures. Eventually you are surrounded by so many half measures that you can no longer see that the heart of the value programmers create comes from programming.

I say, "The beginning of the answer ..." because there is no final answer. The authors in the XP Series have been that and done there, and returned to tell their story. The books in this series are the signposts they have planted along the way: "Here lie dragons," "Scenic drive next 15 km," "Slippery when wet."

Excuse me, I gotta go program.

Titles in the Series

Extreme Programming Applied: Playing to Win, Ken Auer and Roy Miller

Extreme Programming Examined, Giancarlo Succi and Michele Marchesi

Extreme Programming Explained: Embrace Change, Kent Beck

Extreme Programming Explored, William C. Wake

Extreme Programming in Practice, James Newkirk and Robert C. Martin

Extreme Programming Installed, Ron Jeffries, Ann Anderson, and Chet Hendrickson

Planning Extreme Programming, Kent Beck and Martin Fowler

For more information, check out the series Web site at http://www.aw.com/cseng/series/XP/

Questioning Extreme Programming

Pete McBreen

✦✦ Addison-Wesley

Boston • San Francisco • New York • Toronto • Montreal
London • Munich • Paris • Madrid
Capetown • Sydney • Tokyo • Singapore • Mexico City

The publisher offers discounts on this book when ordered in quantity for special sales. For more information, please contact:

Pearson Education Corporate Sales Division
201 W. 103rd Street
Indianapolis, IN 46290
corpsales@pearsontechgroup.com

Visit AW on the Web: www.awprofessional.com

Library of Congress Cataloging-in-Publication Data
McBreen, Pete.
    Questioning Extreme Programming / Pete McBreen.
        p. cm. — (XP series)
    ISBN 0-201-84457-5 (alk. paper)
        1. Computer software—Development. 2. eXtreme programming. I. Title. II. Series.

    QA76.76.D47 .M385 2002
    005.1—dc21

                                                                2002023209

ISBN 0-201-84457-5
Text printed on recycled paper
1 2 3 4 5 6 7 8 9 10—MA—0605040302
First printing, July 2002

To Rod for inspiring me to write
and
To Mr. Angry for helping me find my voice.

Contents

Foreword

Pete and I go way back. I can't remember exactly when we met, but I do remember being impressed with his experience and ability to communicate. When I heard that Pete was writing a book that takes a critical look at XP, I was glad—another set of eyes, particularly those of a thoughtful and self-professed outsider, could only help all of us as we try to improve our own development cultures.

Pete pulled it off. Some of XP's critics fall into shrill, reactionary jeremiads: "It'll never work. You have to design my way, or you'll die. Listen to me. I know how to yell." This book is thorough, thoughtful, and conservative. Pete only makes claims he can back up with experience.

This is not to say I agree with his conclusions. I absolutely do not. XP started out with a fairly limited audience in mind—small teams working on business software. Adventurous pioneers, to use Ken Auer's picturesque metaphor, have carried XP far from its roots:

- Atomic teams as large as 50 (customer side and development side together)
- Teams of teams, often distributed worldwide
- Embedded systems
- Product development—in whichthe customer side has to represent a wide range of interests

Pete claims that the more he looks at XP, the smaller he sees its scope. I see just the opposite. I won't refute his argument point by point—this is a foreword and I'm supposed to be polite. I will suggest that as you read this, you keep in mind one mistake of early XP thinking for which I am entirely responsible—"the customer" doesn't mean *one person*. It means a team, as big as or bigger than the development team.

I trust you will make your own conclusions about the contents of the book. If you agree with Pete's conclusion, you will find here evidence and reasoning aplenty. If you disagree with Pete's conclusion, you will find tough questions that will force you to reexamine your own experience and conclusions. If you don't have an opinion about XP, you will find here a program for coming to your own conclusions. That's why I'm delighted to welcome this book to The XP Series. It's a "make-you-think" book, and XP is supposed to be a "make-you-think" development culture.

Kent Beck
Three Rivers Institute

Preface

Extreme Programming sounds great! Can we do it without changing our process?

When I first heard about Extreme Programming in May 1998, I could see that it was going to be controversial. This was immediately obvious from the wide range of reactions that were expressed regarding two talks given by Kent Beck and Ron Jeffries at a seminar on Developing Software with Objects in Oslo (hosted by Den Norske Dataforening, 13 May 1998). Many developers seemed to be attracted to it, but others in the room challenged the ideas and concepts behind Extreme Programming.

Personally, my reactions were mixed. It sounded like it would be a fun approach to software development and it didn't sound like it was applicable to the kinds of projects that I was involved in. Admittedly, my initial reservations were about how easy it would be to sell the approach, but as I inquired deeper into Extreme Programming, I came to realize that there are fairly stringent preconditions for teams that wish to adopt and use XP. It seems to me that many of the reactions to Extreme Programming can be explained by the fit between these preconditions and the particular project circumstances that a person has experienced.

This book sets out to question Extreme Programming in an attempt to understand and explain the controversy that surrounds Extreme Programming. My goal for this book is to allow you, the reader, to determine if Extreme Programming is applicable and appropriate for your projects, to investigate what lessons can be learned from Extreme Programming, and to enable you to be more reflective about your software development practices.

Before getting down to that I must first explain my biases. As a developer, I am attracted toward the ideas behind XP, mainly because most of the developers I have talked to that have worked on XP projects have really enjoyed the experience. I am also a strong fan of XP-style unit testing and have introduced JUnit (www.junit.org) to many project teams. Although I have never worked on a full XP project, I have worked on a team that initially claimed that it was going to be doing XP, but actually turned out to be doing something that was vaguely related to some of the XP practices.

As much as possible, I have tried to present both sides of the debate surrounding Extreme Programming without getting into the continual flame-fest that discussions on Usenet newsgroups and e-mail lists often contain.

I have written this book as a practical guide for four different audiences:

1. People who are thinking of adopting Extreme Programming
2. People who are resisting the idea of adopting Extreme Programming
3. People who are looking for alternatives to Extreme Programming
4. People who are interested in improving their current software development process

As a practical guide, this book focuses on identifying issues surrounding software development and discussing how Extreme Programming interacts with these issues. Because this is a practical guide, you will not find much in the way of detailed studies and experimental data. This book focuses on clarifying the issues so that you can determine the fit between Extreme Programming and your specific circumstances.

Adopting Extreme Programming

All processes are situational. Software development is not a mechanical process, and as such you will never be able to adopt a process without doing some adapting to fit with your circumstances and team. Before adopting Extreme Programming you need to have a deep understanding of the values that drive it so that the adaptations you make match the overall spirit of XP.

This book looks back at the roots of XP to enable you to understand the underlying software development issues so that you can better assess how XP will fit your organization. This book will also expose you to alternative approaches that may be a better fit.

Resisting Extreme Programming

Extreme Programming is a different kind of software development process. It is one that many programmers actually want to use. All too often, however, this means that some programmers end up pushing the idea of adopting XP when for one reason or another it does not really fit the organization.

This book provides the questions you need to ask to determine whether XP really does fit the needs and circumstances of your organization. Hopefully, it will also allow you to identify the issues with your current process that caused XP to be raised as a potential alternative in the first place. Then, rather than shooting the messenger or dismissing the message, the book asks the question, What can we learn from XP?

Looking for Alternatives to Extreme Programming

Extreme Programming is a great fit for some projects and organizations, but one size does not fit all. There are many other software development approaches, and with all the exposure that Extreme Programming is getting, these alternatives are getting somewhat lost. Using an *agile methodology* does not necessarily mean using Extreme Programming.

Questioning Extreme Programming attempts to uncover the issues that are driving the creation of new approaches to software development. By exposing these issues I hope to spur software developers and their managers to create alternative approaches that build on the strengths of Extreme Programming while incorporating the strengths of the other approaches.

Improving Your Current Software Development Process

Adopting a new software development process can be hard. The organization has to learn how to apply the new process effectively, and there is a transition period when some projects are using the new process while the rest are still using the old process. Sometimes it just makes sense to retain your existing process and try to improve it by dropping parts, changing parts, and adding new parts.

By continually asking the question, What can we learn from XP? this book highlights different ideas that could potentially be applied within the context of a different process. The resulting hybrid will not be XP, but then again, that is not the goal. By adopting the Extreme Programming mind-set of continually reflecting on and tinkering with the process, you open up the possibility of creating your own optimized process.

Why You Should Read This Book

The way that we develop software is changing. Yes, people have always claimed that the information technology industry has been a real driver for change, but until recently that change has only really shown up in the hardware and software. The way that we develop software has been remarkably resistant to change.

Indeed, Watts S. Humphrey spoke for many methodologists in his article "Why Don't They Practice What We Preach?" when he said, "One of the most intractable problems in software is getting engineers to use effective methods." [Humphrey, 2001]

Many proponents of Extreme Programming would claim that the problem is no longer intractable: Lots of programmers would jump at the chance to use XP. Indeed, many developers are very keen to experiment with and try out new ways of developing software. It seems as if developers are beginning to see that things have changed. Jim Highsmith probably summed this up best when he said, "We must challenge our most fundamental assumptions about software development." [Highsmith, 2000, p. 13]

Questioning Extreme Programming invites you to take up that challenge.

Acknowledgments

First I would like to thank Kent Beck, Ward Cunningham, and Ron Jeffries for starting the conversation around Extreme Programming. If nothing else they have managed to make software development methodologies interesting again.

As usual, the team at Addison-Wesley was extremely supportive and enthusiastic about this project: Ross Venables, Mike Hendrickson, et. al. My reviewers seemed particularly gleeful this time, and although one expressed regrets that the book is not the flame-fest material he'd hoped for, all helped me to clarify my thoughts about Extreme Programming: Alastair Handley, Andy Hunt, Dave Thomas, Greg Klafki, Jens Coldewey, Jim Highsmith, Kent Beck, Miroslav Novak, Ron Jeffries, and Rudy Wrench.

Part I

Introduction

Who needs questions?

Is Extreme Programming just hype or is it really a *hyper*productive way of organizing software development? Does Extreme Programming just appeal to the baser instincts of software developers or are there circumstances when it makes sense to focus on business value as expressed by the code as the key deliverable? Are the extremists just trying to tear down the foundations of software engineering or have they really found a way to make small teams more productive?

In the form that these questions are asked, they are hard to answer because they are all polarizing questions that make it hard to see that there are many different shades of gray. Part of the task of questioning XP is to change the conversation away from the early polarizing rhetoric that was used initially to promote Extreme Programming. A classic one was the phrase, "All models are lies," which sparked a lot of heat because it implicitly attacked the idea that you could do design using Unified Modeling Language (UML) diagrams.

In the midst of all of this controversy, though, Extreme Programming has restarted the conversation about software development methodologies. Indeed, the Agile Alliance [http://www.agilealliance.org/] seems to have been triggered, in part at least, by the debates surrounding Extreme Programming. In searching for a way to talk about the differences between the traditional software engineering approaches and the Agile approaches, the Agile Alliance came to the realization that for them, *individuals and interactions* are more important than the *processes and tools.*

It is interesting, therefore, that many of the reactions to Extreme Programming are based on the process and practices used in XP. It is as if the claims that XP is an optimizing process have somehow drowned the more fundamental shift that XP represents—that respect for the individuals and their interactions makes a difference.

The idea of showing respect for the team may be part of the explanation for one really amazing thing about Extreme Programming—it has managed to generate a lot of interest without having a large organization behind it. Yes, the controversial stance adopted by many early proponents of XP probably helped as well, because they challenged the way that most software development was done, and in the process forced people to choose sides.

Chapter 1

XP: Hype or *Hyper*Productive?

"'Extreme Programming:' Act like all you have to do is 'write the program!!" (Jeffries and Hendrickson, 1998)

The most amazing claim I've ever seen for Extreme Programming was in the first talk I heard from Ron Jeffries when he said that the *"Entire team agrees this is the best project they've ever been on."* It is no surprise, then, that some people think XP is a cult. How else can you explain the unanimous applause from the converts? Somehow or other, Extreme Programming has managed to make software development fun for the technical side of the project team.

Small wonder there is a lot of hype surrounding Extreme Programming. It claims to have found a way to remove the drudgery from software development! At the same time, it puts a massive focus on the code: It *is* called Extreme *Programming* after all. By raising the status of the programming activity, it reverses the value system of traditional software development in which mere programmers are looked down on. Indeed, the Extreme Programming community could be said to look down on systems analysts and architects who do not write code.

Much of the controversy surrounding Extreme Programming arises from the fact that it appeals to programmers. In a sense, Extreme Programming is a child of the Internet age. Without the backing of a large organization, it has managed to become a very visible part of the software development landscape. Much of the demand for Extreme Programming is coming from developers who are pushing their managers to be allowed to use XP.

This generates controversy because it is not the way that new software development processes are supposed to be introduced. Managers are supposed to introduce new processes and methods after careful evaluation of the various options presented by different vendors.

Extreme Programming turns all this on its head. The developers know much more about Extreme Programming than their managers, and in their desire to try it out, turn into unpaid evangelists. They even sound like real evangelists because the anecdotal evidence that exists for Extreme Programming sounds too good to be true.

Sample Claims, Counter Claims, and Misinformation

Consider the following:

- ✧ A good XP team is at least six times as productive as a traditional software engineering team.
- ✧ The changed application can be released to production at the end of each two- or three-week iteration.
- ✧ Refactoring means that big design up front is an unnecessary waste of time.
- ✧ Comments in source code are an indication that the code is not clear enough and needs to be refactored.
- ✧ All tests can be automated.
- ✧ All you have to do is write the program.
- ✧ Extreme Programming glorifies "cowboy coding" practices.
- ✧ All models are lies; all that really matters is tested code.
- ✧ Extreme Programming is just glorified hacking.
- ✧ Extreme Programming is setting back the cause of software engineering 30 years.
- ✧ Extreme Programming is misleading and dangerous.
- ✧ If they have to give it a new name to convince the users to get involved in the projects, that is OK, but we have been doing it for years. There is nothing new in XP.

Is There Any Hard Evidence to Support the Claims for XP?

This is the heart of the controversy surrounding Extreme Programming and the reason that the controversy will last for quite a while. Software development is a human activity and, as such, all studies are subject to the Hawthorne effect—the dreaded scourge of all studies on teams and productivity [`http://staff.psy.gla.ac.uk/~steve/hawth.html`].

Once you set out to study a team, the mere fact that you are studying the team changes it enough to make a difference. In the Hawthorne study, most changes had a positive effect on output, *including setting the conditions back to what they were originally* (see preceding URL). These effects were observed in a small team of six manual workers during a period of five years and, although the study has been challenged because of the small number of people studied and the fact that two workers were replaced during the study, the study highlights the importance of experimental design.

This is very relevant when studying Extreme Programming, because in software development, motivation and morale matter. Indeed, some claim that people factors are the best predictor of project outcome [Cockburn, 2002, p. 43]. When a team has lobbied for and eventually adopted Extreme Programming, of course they are going to do their utmost to make it successful. Similarly, a team that has had Extreme Programming imposed on them against their wishes will resist it and prove that it does not work.

Although it might be possible to find some software developers who are neutral about Extreme Programming for use in a study, it is unlikely that they would remain neutral for long. Developers cannot remain neutral because Extreme Programming drastically changes what they do on an hour-by-hour, minute-by-minute basis. *Pair Programming* and *Test First Design*, to take two examples, are really different. Instead of sitting alone to write the code and then later figuring out how to test it, developers collaborate in pairs to write all production code and start by writing a test case, running it to prove that the test case fails, and only then coding the functionality to make that test case pass. *Culture shock* is too mild a term to use for the difference between traditional software development and Extreme Programming practices. As such, it is very hard to find developers who are neutral because it changes what they do so much.

As an aside, even if you could find an appropriate experimental group, finding a control group could be equally hard. The problem is that of the John Henry effect, in which the control group pulls out all the stops to outperform the experimental group.

Should We Ask for Comparative Studies?

Although opponents of Extreme Programming are always asking for studies about the effectiveness of XP, it is interesting to note that there are no real studies that support any methodology. There are no comparative studies that have ever taken place on reasonable-size projects. Indeed, it is hard to trust any of the studies in the software engineering field because they were either carried out a long time ago or because the numbers come from a small study that lasted a few weeks.

✧ Studies that were carried out more than ten years ago are suspect because of the dramatic improvements in hardware and software tools over the years. Personally, I find that object-oriented programming at an interactive workstation is qualitatively different from the old days of batch compiles in low-level languages, when we were lucky to get three or four compilation runs a day.

✧ Small short-duration studies are suspect because they are dominated by short-term learning effects, mainly because they are constrained to using novices. This is a problem because novices use different strategies than experts, and when experts switch to a new way of working, they experience a larger drop in performance than novices. These two factors make it dangerous to extrapolate long-term expert performance from that of novices.

So what studies could be done? One that could be done, but is very unlikely to happen, is a comparative study of several approaches to developing, evolving, and maintaining an application for two or more years. The application would have to be complex enough to need at least a team of six developers, and you would need several teams using each approach to smooth out the differences between the capabilities and the performance of the individuals on the teams. For added information, the study should cover a range of development languages and platforms, but that would drastically raise the cost of the study.

Anecdotal Evidence Is Not Necessarily Bad

Sometimes it seems as if the software engineering community does not value anecdotal evidence, even when there are many projects reporting essentially the same results. Indeed, it sometimes seems as if the results reported from a small controlled study are valued much more than contradictory results reported from software development projects. Researchers, it would seem, have a different value system than practitioners. Researchers are used to applying the scientific method to find out how things work, whereas practitioners are used to dealing with marketing claims and counterclaims.

Practitioners welcome anecdotal evidence as a means of sorting out the various claims and counterclaims. Anecdotal evidence is useful because it provides some context that enables the results to be interpreted. Yes, it does not represent a controlled study, but real projects are not controlled studies either. More important, anecdotal evidence is a great counter to the problem of researchers extrapolating ideas from a single study, or converting study results into unquestionable dogma.

A good example of this is the unquestioned faith that the cost of change rises dramatically (exponentially?) over time. Very many projects manage to develop incrementally, and there are plenty of examples of defects that were trivial and inexpensive to fix, so we have a case of anecdotal evidence contradicting research results. Some of the debates about the applicability of Extreme Programming arise out of this discrepancy between anecdotal evidence from projects and research results.

Reevaluating the Cost of Change

A study that definitely should be reevaluated is the oft-quoted study about the exponential cost of change on projects. The original source of this is Boehm's *Software Engineering Economics* [Boehm, 1981, p. 40–41], but the data refers to large projects in the 1980s and earlier. Kent Beck makes the point in *Extreme Programming Explained* [Beck, 2000, p. 21–25] that the cost of change may not rise dramatically over time. Indeed, he calls it "the technical premise of XP."

Getting the numbers to reevaluate the cost of change will be hard. The problem is that the software development practices you use affect the cost of change, and these in turn are influenced by your expectations about the cost and likelihood of change. We also have to remember that software development is an economic activity and that the costs of each strategy for dealing with change have to be evaluated on a per-project basis.

⋄ Should the team try to do exhaustive analysis and design in flexibility to support all foreseeable future changes with simple configuration changes?

- ✧ Should the team do enough analysis to understand the likely points that need to be changed and spend extra money making those parts more flexible?
- ✧ Should the team write the application so that dependencies are minimized and it is easy to change any part of the code when necessary?
- ✧ Should the team focus on getting the current version shipped, knowing that any future changes will be paid for out of a different budget?

All these strategies and more are perfectly viable in the correct context. The hard part is deciding what context applies to your project.

All Processes Are Situational

There is no such thing as the "one best way" to develop software. Indeed, it is a mistake to think there is anything like a "best practice," as far as software development is concerned. As I have mentioned in *Software Craftsmanship* [McBreen, 2002], the idea of "one best way" and the concept of "best practices" are holdovers from scientific management and have no place in software development.

This does not mean that developers should do whatever they feel like doing, but developers should choose an appropriate set of practices based on the current circumstances. It is highly unlikely that any codified rule that states that a team should use a particular "best practice" is ever going to be appropriate for the majority of projects. There is just too much diversity in projects and teams. All practices in software development are situational, and their appropriateness depends on a multitude of factors, including the team, the organizational environment, and the project.

The problem with evaluating any approach to software development, and the reason for much of the controversy surrounding XP, is the essential irreproducibility of results. Just because one team was successful with an approach on a particular project does not mean that another team would be successful with the same approach on a different project.

Do You Need Process Improvement or Process Change?

When we start questioning Extreme Programming, we first need to understand why we are asking the questions. Although it can be interesting to seek to understand a different approach, the questions only have any real meaning when applied to your own situation. You could be interested because you are wondering whether to adopt Extreme Programming, or maybe you are interested because you want to see what lessons can be learned from Extreme Programming that can be applied to your current approach.

My approach to this is first to understand whether the existing process is broken and needs to be replaced or whether it is working and just needs to be improved. This distinction is very important, because the costs of these two different actions are drastically different.

Changing to a different process is very expensive for an organization, and can be hazardous for teams because key team members may reject the new approach. Hence, I only consider adopting a new approach when there is considerable evidence that the existing approach is broken and cannot easily be fixed.

Signs That Your Process Is Broken

There are some very simple signs that your process is broken and needs to be fixed:

- ⬥ Your projects fail to deliver a working application, are late, or only ship through heroic efforts.
- ⬥ Surprises keep on showing up late in the project (delays, cost overruns, defective software).
- ⬥ Developers leave the project before it is completed. (Very few people want to bail out of a winning team. If people are bailing out, something is wrong.)
- ⬥ Team members argue more than they smile.

Using these simple signs, it is very easy to determine whether a process is broken. In most cases, the signs will be that your process is broken. If the statistics are to be believed [`http://www.pm2go.com/sample_research/chaos_1994_1.asp`], projects that finish on time without stressing out the team are in the minority. The astounding conclusion you have to draw from this is either that most processes are broken or, as Humphrey suggests, "software development teams are not using effective methods." [Humphrey, 2001]

Understanding Software Development Processes

This depressing thought that most processes are broken brings me back to Jim Highsmith's remark that "*We must challenge our most fundamental assumptions about software development.*" [Highsmith, 2000, p. 13] After all, nobody would deliberately design a software development process to demoralize a team, be unpredictable until nearly the end, and have a low probability of delivering on time.

Resolving this puzzle requires us to think eitherthat teams are not using the processes that exist, as Humphrey suggests, or that the circumstances have changed and that the old processes no longer apply, as Highsmith suggests. Although there is some evidence to support the idea that project teams are just not using software development processes correctly, this is too easy an answer.

Personally, I do not think it is useful to lay the blame on the project teams. In part, this is because blaming the team does not open many avenues for improving the situation. Yes, in the longer term we can change the skills and the abilities of our software development teams, but I have already written about that [McBreen, 2002].

In the short term, a more effective avenue to explore is that of changing our assumptions about software development. After all, if it turns out that people and their interactions are in fact more important than processes and tools, then aligning our processes with this insight would give immediate benefits.

This book attempts to explore our assumptions about software development by questioning Extreme Programming. By looking into the details of XP, you will be able to see where the assumptions XP makes are different from your own. You are likely to discover a difference between what you think is important and the items that XP assumes are important.

XP Is Optimized for Predictable Pace Delivery

Extreme Programming is set up to give predictable, sustained, and sustainable delivery of software in an environment that respects all members of the team. It may sound strange given the various claims that have been made about improving productivity, but XP is not concerned with going fast. It assumes that a predictable, sustained pace is more valuable. This predictability brings with it an uncertainty about the scope of the delivery. So, in a way, Extreme Programming offers an alternative to the more common predictable scope but uncertain delivery date projects.

Another key assumption underpinning XP is that valuable software will be maintained and extended indefinitely, and that the same team will work on the software for the entire duration. XP assumes that the team will remain intact throughout the project and that a handoff to another team is unlikely. Yes, the team will experience turnover, and the size of the team may change as the demand for new features changes, but continuity will be maintained.

XP also assumes that as the software is used, completely new, unpredictable requirements will emerge that have to be handled by the software. Sometimes these new requirements will take the application in a completely new direction. These new features should be handled just as predictably and sustainably as any other expected new-feature request.

Understanding the Controversy Around XP

The assumptions that XP makes are similar to those made by organizations that create software products. They are vastly different from the assumptions made by traditional software projects that assemble a team, deliver an application to a maintenance department, and then disband the team. These teams want to deliver as fast as possible, be as productive as possible, and then move on to other challenges. They do not want to get stuck in maintenance.

The mismatch in assumptions is where much of the controversy is grounded. XP is optimized for a different outcome using strategies that are inappropriate for the traditional project-driven approach. Without looking at the underlying assumptions, it is easy to end up criticizing XP for not doing something that it has minimized through careful optimization.

Is XP an Option for You?

Will Extreme Programming turn out to be just hype when tried in your organization? Or will it make your team hyperproductive? From this distance it is hard to tell. To get an answer, we need to look more closely at the details of Extreme Programming and other approaches so that we can see how different methodologies approach the problems that development teams face.

Summary

✧ Most software development processes are broken. Projects succeed to the extent that teams adjust their process to match the project realities.

✧ Many software developers are attracted to Extreme Programming.

✧ The controversy surrounding Extreme Programming continues to grow as its ideas increase in popularity.

✧ All processes are situational. What works for one team may not work for another.

✧ Changing processes is hard. Attempt it only when the benefits massively outweigh the costs.

✧ Extreme Programming makes different assumptions about what is important in software development.

✧ Extreme Programming is set up to give predictable, sustained, and sustainable delivery of software in an environment that respects all members of the team.

✧ XP is optimized for a different outcome using strategies that are inappropriate for the traditional project-driven approach.

Part II

What Is a Methodology?

"There is more than one way to do it."
—Larry Wall's Perl slogan

In all of the controversy surrounding Extreme Programming, we need to remember that it is just one way of organizing a team to deliver an application. There are many other competing ways to develop software.

Although there are many different definitions of methodology, in the end they all come down to the same thing. A software development methodology is how an organization chooses to organize people and resources to create and to maintain applications. Unfortunately, this definition doesn't really say much about what a methodology *is*, rather it just states the overall purpose—that of creating and maintaining applications.

Most approaches focus on the first part of the definition—that of creating the application. Few approaches have much to say about the maintenance part, even though it appears that more money is spent on supporting and maintaining applications than is spent on creating them in the first place.

The other challenge around understanding and defining what a methodology is has been explained by Alistair Cockburn in *Agile Software Development* [Cockburn, 2002, p. 14]. A methodology has to be tailored toward the different audiences that will be using it. Beginners are looking for a detailed sequence of steps to follow to guarantee success. Intermediates are looking for a range of strategies to use at different times in a project, whereas an expert is primarily interested in discovering the artifacts and checkpoints that the methodology requires.

To cut through all of this (and to make this book short enough to be readable), I will look at a small subset of approaches and focus on the idea of methodology as a way of optimizing the work on a project to safeguard the organization's values. All methodologies are designed to give optimal results. The things the methodology optimizes are the key to understanding what is important for that methodology. The approaches that will be looked at are

- ✧ The traditional software engineering approach
- ✧ The Unified Process
- ✧ Open Source

and the Agile approaches:

- ✧ Adaptive Software Development
- ✧ Crystal
- ✧ Dynamic Systems Development Method (DSDM)
- ✧ Feature-Driven Development
- ✧ Pragmatic Programming
- ✧ Scrum
- ✧ Extreme Programming

Looking at what a methodology optimizes enables the discussion to focus on what is important within the methodology. Although the artifacts, deliverables, and checkpoints will vary between all of these different methodologies, there is one underlying constant: All methodologies are designed to optimize the production of the items it considers important.

Your task in reading about these methodologies is to determine how the values of your organization match the values expressed in each methodology. Does Extreme Programming optimize the aspects that are important to your organization? Does your organization value the things that Extreme Programming is optimized to deliver?

Chapter 2

What Do Methodologies Optimize?

All methodologies are based on fear.
—Kent Beck (Beck, 2000, p. 165)

Are all methodologies optimized for risk mitigation? I don't think so. Kent Beck's sound bite that methodologies are based on fear is an obvious overstatement, but it does neatly frame many of the conversations surrounding Extreme Programming. It also positions Extreme Programming as the macho, fearless approach to software development and has the hidden implication that only wimps would choose to use a more traditional software development process. Small wonder, then, that Extreme Programming has generated such controversy.

Why the Focus on Fear?

To understand this we need to look at the background of Extreme Programming. Although it is not very evident in much of the Java-centric literature that surrounds Extreme Programming, it owes most of its heritage to ideas from the Smalltalk world.

Ward Cunningham documented many of the Extreme Programming practices in his EPISODES pattern language [Vlissides, 1996, p. 371–388] from his experiences on the WyCash Smalltalk project. Indeed, it appears that many of the Extreme Programming practices arose from the way that Ward and Kent worked together during the 1980s in the Smalltalk environment.

I'm directing your attention toward Smalltalk because even in the 1980s, Smalltalk had powerful, expressive class libraries and a forgiving, flexible, powerful, and productive development environment. The Smalltalk environment encourages developers to be fearless because it is so forgiving [Baetjer, 1998, p. 101]. It really encourages incremental design and development because you know that there is no way that you can "paint yourself into a corner." (This is a reference to the silent black-and-white comedy movies in which doorways always got papered over and painters always ended up in the corner of a room.)

In sharp contrast to this, I distinctly remember trying to get stuff right the first time when working in C++ in the early 1990s because it was such a pain to change things later. Renaming methods and classes to make them more expressive was not something we consciously thought of because it was so hard to do. We knew that if we made a mistake, we were going to paint ourselves into a corner!

Although Extreme Programming has grown beyond its roots in the Smalltalk culture, it still embodies the idea that, given good tools, programs are easy to change and that applications can be understood by reading the source code. This is in sharp contrast to the traditional software development experience that programs are notoriously hard to change and the code is so convoluted that separate documentation is necessary to make any sense of the application.

Extreme Programming assumes that code is all that matters, because enough people have had the experience that well-written code is easy to understand and modify. Traditional software development assumes that documentation is essential because enough people have suffered from undocumented, unmaintainable code. Seen from the other set of assumptions, XP is irresponsible and will leave behind more undocumented, unmaintainable code, whereas the traditional approach wastes time by forcing developers to write documentation that nobody will ever read.

Extreme Programming sees the traditional approach as being overburdened by deliverables and artifacts resulting from a fear of failure. In the words of Tom DeMarco,

> *[Process standardization] tries to avoid all chance of failure by having key decisions made by a guru class (those who set the standards) and carried out mechanically by the regular folk. As defense against failure, standard process is a kind of armor. The more worried you are about*

failure, the more armor you put on. But armor always has a side effect of reducing mobility. The overarmored organization has lost the ability to move quickly. [DeMarco, 2001, p. 110]

Methodologies Record Bad Experiences on Projects

One way of looking at a methodology is that it is the way an organization armors itself against past failures. Although good organizations celebrate and learn from failure, in practically every organization, making the same mistake twice is a career-limiting move. Seen in this light, what a methodology does is make it hard to repeat dumb, career-limiting mistakes.

In some organizations, this methodology is carefully documented and recorded; in others, it is just a kind of oral tradition. However, every organization has its own version of "the way we do things around here." Sometimes, the way an organization does things is close to the way a published methodology suggests things should be done; at other times, it is completely homegrown. The bottom line, though, is that every organization has a way that it prefers to organize projects.

In most cases, "the way we do things around here" reflects the interests and needs of the organization's managers and project sponsors to coordinate and control the various development projects. Methodologies are the way that these key members of the organization make sure that they do not repeat past mistakes. Most (all?) elements of a methodology are there to allow these key people to see what is happening in a project and to compare one project with another.

In traditional methodologies, the needs of the development team could easily be seen as secondary considerations. To quote Tom DeMarco,

> *In my experience, standard processes for knowledge work are almost always empty at the center. . . . I see design standards that don't tell you how to come up with a good design (only how to write it down), . . . testing standards that don't tell you how to invent a test that is worth running.* [DeMarco, 2001, p. 108]

Small wonder, then, that Extreme Programming complains that the traditional approaches are based on fear. It is as if the traditional approaches have been optimized to minimize the risk of making a mistake, and even if the cost is that the project proceeds at a glacially slow pace, that is preferable to making a mistake.

- -

How Do Methodologies Record Bad Experiences?

Every methodology calls for the team to write down the requirements because everybody knows that if they are not written down, the team could go off track and deliver the wrong thing. Methodologies differ regarding the exact form their written requirements will take, but each form is influenced by previous failures. Organizations that have in the past been burned by vague requirements will favor methodologies that have very formal requirements practices. Similarly, organizations that have been burned by analysis paralysis will favor methodologies that allow development to get started with only vague requirements.

Historically, many Smalltalk projects have run into trouble because the development team tried to build too much flexibility into the application. Rather than build the application, team members often ended up building a framework to build applications. Small wonder, then, that Extreme Programming focuses on simple design and not adding anything that isn't needed by the immediate requirements. The organization benefits from this because it has an easy way to detect whether a solution is overgeneralized and not focused on immediate delivery.

Similarly, Smalltalk programs can suffer from runtime errors because there is little in the way of compile time checking for coding errors. To alleviate this problem, the Smalltalk community has developed a culture of doing extensive unit-level or developer testing to ensure that all methods are implemented correctly. This is codified in the Unit Testing practice of Extreme Programming. The organization benefits from this because it has an easy way to detect whether sufficient developer testing has taken place (runtime errors means there hasn't been enough) and the delivered applications have fewer mistakes in them.

What Do Developers Look for in a Process?

After looking at how methodologies meet the needs of an organization, it is instructive to look at how methodologies can be optimized to meet the needs of developers. After all, it would be nice if a software development methodology actually assisted the software developers in creating the software, instead of making them feel like it just gets in the way.

Few software developers are worried about making dumb mistakes, because the process of learning to be a developer involves making lots of small, dumb mistakes. Indeed, many programming tools are just automated ways of spotting typos and misspellings.

Software developers are motivated by the desire to create applications that they can be proud of—something that they can use to show how good they are. Their motivation is more based on pride. They want to excel. This is the reason that developers want to use Extreme Programming and the other Agile methods. Programmers feel that the Agile methods enable them to deliver working software.

Above all, software developers want a process that allows them to deliver great software. Many want to be involved in all stages and aspects of the project, and above all want to be allowed to write code. Developers want a process with minimum bureaucracy that allows them to correct any mistakes that are made quickly. They want a process that reflects the way that software is really developed, not a hollow process that rigidly specifies how to document inappropriate deliverables without giving any guidance regarding how to create great software.

Experience, Talent, and Tacit Knowledge

A common criticism of Extreme Programming and the other Agile approaches is that they rely too heavily on the expertise of the developers in the team. Indeed, Barry Boehm has cautioned that the Agile approaches rely *"on the tacit knowledge embodied in the team, rather than writing the knowledge down in plans"* [Boehm, 2002, p. 65]. He contrasts this with what he calls the "plan-driven" approaches that make this tacit knowledge explicit in written plans and documentation. Boehm's concern is that

> *Without premium people, however, you're more likely to get a design-by-committee mess. A significant consideration here is the unavoidable statistic that 49.9999 percent of the world's software developers are below average.* [Boehm, 2002, p. 65]

The question about tacit knowledge was explored by Nonaka and Takeuchi in their book *The Knowledge Creating Company*. They point out the fact that

> *. . . the interaction between tacit and explicit knowledge is performed by the individual, not by the organization itself. . . . the socialization mode [sharing of tacit knowledge] starts by building a team whose members share their experiences and mental models. The externalization mode [converting tacit to explicit knowledge] is triggered by successive rounds of meaningful dialogue. Metaphors and analogies, which enable team*

members to articulate their own perspectives and thereby reveal hidden tacit knowledge that is otherwise hard to communicate, are often used in dialogue. [Nonaka, 1995, p. 225]

All software development processes—Agile or plan driven—rely on tacit knowledge. The difference between them is merely one of degree. Agile methods embrace and even celebrate the tacit knowledge that individuals bring to the team, whereas more traditional approaches worry about the risk that this essential knowledge is not written down and made explicit.

As far as needing above-average people, Boehm's assessment is dubious. External knowledge is not better than tacit knowledge. Indeed, as Nonaka has pointed out, to make effective use of externalized knowledge, a person has to internalize that knowledge and make it tacit. Nonaka's viewpoint is that a team has to come together and share their tacit knowledge by communicating. Yes, a small portion of this knowledge will eventually get written down, but what matters is the sharing of the tacit knowledge.

Knowledge that is externalized into documentation is useful only if someone can find it and, having found it, actually reads it. Knowing where to look is a major problem because nobody has the time to read 1,000 or more pages of documentation. The solution is not to write more documentation, but to create a learning environment in which knowledge is shared. You want to set up a collaborative environment that is conducive to learning so that the entire development team shares their knowledge, tacit or otherwise. This is true whether your team is above or below average. You want your team to learn and improve as the project progresses.

You will also want to get as much talent into your team as you can. You want your team to be experience heavy [McBreen, 2002, p. 145]. If you are going to use a small Agile team, enthusiastic beginners are useful, but they have to be in the minority. Yes, this may not be a solution for every project, but this is not the problem that we are trying to solve. What you need is to have your projects be successful, and for that all you need are five or ten talented developers: some with broad experience and some who are relative beginners.

Heavy, Rigorous, Tailorable, Light, Minimal, and Agile Methodologies

An interesting aspect to consider is that the elements of the methodology exist to constrain the behaviors of the project team. They are there to make sure every team does what some other teams didn't do in the past. In this way every methodology can be seen as a constraint that is placed on the project team.

The problem with all of this, as pointed out by Tom DeMarco in his keynote speech at OOPSLA 2001, is that we do not have any mechanism for removing bits from our methodologies. Each new mistake encourages us to add more things to the methodology,[1] but our successes do not encourage us to lighten the methodology load on the next project.

Many developers feel that a heavyweight methodology is a hindrance to delivering the application. They feel that the methodology hinders rather than assists development. In these circumstances a project team may start to work off-process while continuing to espouse the original methodology. Normally, what happens is that the organization remains tolerant of the variation while it is successful, but reacts by reimposing the original methodology with increased discipline if the off-process project fails to deliver.

At the same time, however, there is a realization by many organizations that smaller projects can benefit from having an appropriate-size methodology. One reaction to this is the idea of methodology frameworks that can be tailored to suit a particular set of project circumstances. The idea being that, for large projects, most of the elements of the methodology are mandatory, but for smaller projects only a subset of the elements are mandatory, and the rest is optional based on the risks that the project is facing. The idea is that the organization trades off the risk of making a mistake against the risk that the project will take too long or cost too much. In other words, sometimes it makes sense to optimize the process to reduce the schedule or to reduce costs.

---

1. "Software: The New Realities," at the OOPSLA conference October 16, 2001, in Tampa, FL.

Another reaction has been to create methodologies that are suited to smaller teams and "Internet time." Originally these were called *lightweight methodologies* to contrast with the heavyweight approaches that were crushing teams and projects. Another name that was used for a time was *minimal methodologies*, but this name never really caught on. (Possibly because it did not give the right message. The implication was that you were using a minimal methodology because you could not afford to use a real methodology.) The name that seems to have stuck, however, is that of *Agile methodologies*.

By starting off from a small-team perspective, the Agile methodologies have been able to focus on a different set of outcomes compared with the large-project methodologies. These Agile approaches are optimized for different results. The next two chapters look at the motivations behind these Agile methodologies and compare and contrast these motivations with the other methodologies.

Summary

- Software developers want a process that allows them to deliver great software.
- "Painting yourself into a corner" actually turns out to be hard to do when using incremental development.
- Extreme Programming embodies the idea that, given good tools, programs are easy to change and applications can be understood by reading the source code.
- With traditional methodologies, the needs of the development team could easily be seen as secondary considerations.
- It is instructive to look at how well methodologies are optimized to meet the needs of developers.
- All software development processes—Agile or plan driven—rely on tacit knowledge. The difference between them is merely one of degree.
- Every element of a methodology exists to constrain the behaviors of the project team.
- An alternative to heavyweight methodologies is the idea of methodology frameworks that can be tailored to suit a particular set of

project circumstances. Unfortunately, few teams have the skills or experience to tailor these frameworks successfully.

✧ By starting off from a small-team perspective, the Agile methodologies have been able to focus on a different set of outcomes compared with the large-project methodologies.

Chapter 3

What Are XP Projects Scared Of?

A popular, successful software development methodology will upset a lot of people.

Extreme Programming is an interesting approach because it evolved out of successful software development practices in the Smalltalk world. As such, it pays much more attention than any of the other approaches to what developers do on a project. It also is mainly focused on fears that developers have about projects as opposed to fears that the organization has about projects.

One way of characterizing XP would be to say that it was created by developers to allow them to do what they want to do, while reassuring the organization that the project will deliver successfully. Although this could be seen as an uncharitable interpretation of XP, it turns out that the fears that developers have and the fears an organization has about a project are reasonably aligned.

XP Was Created to Address Project Risks

As Kent Beck states in the opening sentence of *Extreme Programming Explained*, "The basic problem of software development is risk." [Beck, 2000, p. 3] The examples of risk are instructive:

- ✧ Schedule slips
- ✧ Project canceled
- ✧ System goes sour
- ✧ Defect rate

- ✧ Business misunderstood
- ✧ Business changes
- ✧ False feature rich
- ✧ Staff turnover

Each of these risks is grounded in developer fears.

Developers really fear schedule slips because they are high profile and are never forgotten by the organization. Plus, developers feel really stupid having to explain last-minute slips. Canceled projects are a real drag because they, too, are never forgotten by the organization. Developers also fear cancelation because it creates a gap in the resume, and because developers never want to be part of the conversation that starts, "I see you worked on the project that flushed $10 million."

Similarly, developers are scared of projects when the system goes sour and/or has a high defect rate. Both mean lots of stress and long hours, marathon "debugging" sessions stepping through incomprehensible code, and having to explain to the organization why major portions of the new system are going to have to be rewritten.

Misunderstanding the business is a real fear for developers because it is a great way to get into a really awkward situation. Not only do the developers have to explain why the mistake occurred, but they also have to go back and fix it.

Business changes are terrifying because there is nothing worse for a development team than to be told that the software they have lavished most of their waking hours on is irrelevant.

False feature rich is something that developers get scared of only as they gain experience. Early on in their careers, developers just love to add cool stuff into applications, but eventually every developer ends up in a situation where he has to explain to a project lead why he wasted time on the cool feature when there was more important stuff to work on.

Staff turnover itself is not really something that developers fear, but they are scared of being on a really great project team and then finding that conditions deteriorate to the point that they start looking for work elsewhere.

But Project Risks Are Symptoms, Not the Disease

In reviewing a draft of this book, Andy Hunt (personal communication, February 2002) pointed out that the risks associated with various adverse outcomes are just the symptoms. Project teams could easily go crazy trying to catalog, quantify, and mitigate all of the myriad risks that even a small project faces. Instead, what teams need to do is pay attention to the disease that is causing all the symptoms. Looking at this pragmatically, teams have a much simpler challenge. The disease affecting projects is two headed: ignorance and haste.

Ignorance is difficult to treat because it is hard to admit to our own ignorance. Reframing the problem as "how to be successful with only partial knowledge" makes the conversation more palatable. By talking about partial knowledge environments, we enable a team to talk about the research, investigation of prior art, and learning involved in successfully delivering an application. This is in marked contrast to most teams, which seem to specialize in reinventing wheels and ignoring previous work.

Haste is an endemic problem in the software industry. Project teams are nearly always pressed for time and hence end up ignoring prior work because the team does not take the time to do the necessary research and learning. The problem with haste has been described by Tom DeMarco as a consequence of what he calls *Lister's Law:* "People under time pressure don't *think* faster." [DeMarco, 2001, p. 50] When teams are under time pressure, the team members make sure that they look busy, even though they know that what they should really be doing is taking the time to research and think about what they are doing.

Unfortunately, haste makes the effects of ignorance even worse. When faced with partial knowledge, developers can either make assumptions based on their own experience or they can ask questions and do research. In all too many organizations, the developers have been trained to make assumptions. True, the training department does not put on a course called "Assumptions 101," but by word and deed developers are encouraged to keep on working and to ask only really important questions.

Interestingly, Extreme Programming addresses this two-headed disease very effectively. Requiring the customer to work as an integral part of the development team makes it easier for developers to ask questions, and many of the practices are aimed at discouraging developers from making assumptions. By colocating the team, XP encourages the entire team to ask questions rather than make assumptions. This goes a long way toward addressing the problem of delivering quality applications in the face of partial knowledge, because by involving the entire team there is less chance that important issues will be overlooked.

The problem of haste is addressed by talking about the concept of a sustainable pace and small releases. Indeed, the entire planning process in Extreme Programming addresses the issue of haste by the way that it divides up the responsibility for the planning between the developers and the customer [Beck and Fowler, 2001]. Overall, XP addresses haste through a predictable, sustained, and sustainable pace.

Summary

Although Kent Beck [Beck, 2000, p. 3] claims that the basic problem is risk, the underlying problem is that many projects are expected to make haste in the face of partial knowledge.

- ◇ One way of characterizing XP would be to say that it was created by developers to allow them to do what they want to do, while reassuring the organization that the project will deliver successfully.
- ◇ Developers really fear schedule slips because they are high profile and are never forgotten by the organization.
- ◇ The disease affecting projects is two headed: ignorance and haste.
- ◇ Ignorance is difficult to treat because it is hard to admit to our own ignorance.
- ◇ Haste is an endemic problem in the software industry.
- ◇ Unfortunately, haste makes the effects of ignorance even worse.
- ◇ XP addresses these underlying problems by enabling developers to take the time to learn what they need to know while reassuring the organization about the eventual success of the project through predictable, sustained, and sustainable delivery.

Chapter 4

What Do Other Methodologies Consider Important?

Few methods pay enough attention to team quality-of-life issues.

It is very hard to generalize about methodologies. Yes, you can create interesting sound bites, but although interesting, these sound bites do not shape the behaviors or people on projects. Take, for example, the saying that *the basic problem in software development is risk*. All too many projects do little if any risk management or risk mitigation, so it does not seem that many projects are managed as if the basic problem is risk. Indeed, it seems as if many projects are completely unconscious of the possibility of failure.

Whatever criteria are used for identifying important project outcomes, different projects and methodologies will pay attention to some outcomes and ignore others. This does, however, provide a useful way to compare and contrast the different approaches. By looking in detail at the outcomes the various methodologies are optimized to deliver, we can get a better idea about the applicability of the methodologies to different situations.

To put this all in context, Extreme Programming is optimized to deliver the following outcomes:

⬧ A predictable, sustained, and sustainable pace in the face of changing requirements

- ✧ A collaborative, supportive environment for developers
- ✧ Enhancement of the skills and knowledge of the development team

Although it would be possible to claim that Extreme Programming considers productivity and quality important, both of these are just secondary outcomes. As Ron Jeffries stated when reviewing an early draft of this book (personal communication, February 2002), "the point is steering, not going at full speed." Extreme Programming pays a lot of attention to code quality, but this is necessary to gain a predictable, sustainable pace. It does not, however, pay the fanatical attention to quality that is required when developing safety- and life-critical systems, so it would be incorrect to state that XP is optimized for quality.

In this discussion about the different approaches I will focus on application development in its many forms: in-house applications, outsourced projects, and shrink-wrapped application software. The myriad other forms of software development—embedded systems, software components, application suites, customization of package software, and package software—may get mentioned in passing, but the focus is on mainstream software development.

What Do Software Engineering Projects Consider Important?

In this category I include the software development approaches that are most heavily influenced by the software engineering paradigm. These approaches can be characterized by their use of traditional analysis, design, programming, and testing activities. Although each approach may place different emphasis on each of these activities, conversations with practitioners always mention these four activities as distinct and distinguishable.

These distinctions date back to the early days of software engineering. Initially it was thought that the reason why projects were experiencing trouble was that the programming part wasn't being done properly. This gave rise to the era of structured programming, which soon led to the realization that the implementation activities were not the real cause of project failures. Attention then shifted upstream, and a variety of approaches were created that sought to rectify problems in the design activities. Jackson Structured Design [Jackson, 1995] is just one example of this kind of approach that demonstrated that the design activities were not the main cause of the problems either. Shortly afterward, we got some structured analysis or structured analysis and design approaches that demonstrated it wasn't really an analysis problem either. Shortly after that, depending on how you read history, attention shifted to either the project management aspects of projects or to an integrated, whole life cycle approach to software development.

One remarkable thing about this interpretation of history is that, in all of it, testing never really showed up as an area on which to focus much attention. This is interesting from the viewpoint of the Agile methodologies, which place a lot of emphasis on testing. And it is especially interesting from the viewpoint of Extreme Programming, which places a massive emphasis on testing and testability.

Another remarkable thing about this interpretation is how stable the categories have remained. Analysis, design, programming, and testing are still seen as distinct activities, and warning bells sound whenever there is any blurring between these distinctions.

With all of that said, it is time to look at the different software engineering approaches.

Traditional Waterfall Projects

Although it is hard to find people who actively promote this venerable old approach, the waterfall life cycle still dominates much of the conversation about software development. Analysis, design, programming, and testing are still talked about as separate phases during a project. Pay and respect drop the lower down the waterfall a person is located, with lowly testers typically near the bottom of the heap (although they might be classed slightly higher than maintenance programmers).

Waterfall projects consider the following aspects of a project to be very important:

- ⬥ Efficiency through specialization
- ⬥ Detailed project plans to enable performance tracking
- ⬥ Comprehensive documentation to enable auditability and traceability

Efficiency is important in waterfall projects because of the high cost of rework associated with this type of project, as shown by the exponential cost of change in Boehm's *Software Engineering Economics*

[Boehm, 1981]. This is the reason that the waterfall clearly delineates the phases based on the main software development activities. By delaying starting design until analysis is complete and verified, the chances of having to rework the design as the result of newly discovered requirements are minimized. Similarly, programming starts only after design is complete—when all the interactions between all the modules have been identified and designed.

Specialization of staff into different roles to support the different phases is claimed to promote efficiency by reducing the number of skills a person needs. A systems analyst can focus on getting good at eliciting requirements and understanding what the users need. A designer can specialize in creating designs to meet the requirements without having to worry too much about the implementation technology. Programmers and testers can similarly play their part without needing to know too much about the other jobs in a project. This classic division of labor on the project promotes overall efficiency because programming and testing are relatively low-skill tasks on waterfall projects.

The old joke about software projects being 90 percent complete for 90 percent of the time means that waterfall projects pay attention to planning and tracking the progress of the project. With clear milestones between phases and known dependencies between deliverables, it is easy to display a waterfall project on a Program Evaluation Review Technique (PERT) chart. Hence, the structure of the project makes it amenable for review by the PERT, which neatly addresses the fear of not knowing the status of the project.

Comprehensive documentation is important, so that at the end of the project it is possible to justify the overall costs and hence demonstrate that the project has indeed been efficient. This supports the tracking of the project because it makes everything available for external review, and addresses the inefficiency concerns because it means that you never have to waste time tracking people down to ask them a question. You can just look it up in the documentation. A side benefit of all of this documentation is traceability. You can easily explain to an auditor why a particular feature cost as much as it did, and prove to an auditor that the feature is implemented correctly.

In a stable world in which predictable delivery is more important than quick delivery, the waterfall approach is an efficient, minimal-cost solution. It minimizes costs by avoiding inefficient rework and by providing detailed specifications so that each succeeding phase can use lesser-skilled (and hence cheaper) staff.

Ad Hoc Projects

Although it may be unfair to list the ad hoc approach under software engineering projects, this approach is very similar to the waterfall approach. Ad hoc projects recognize the same roles, activities, and phases, but are typically much more informal. Often the roles overlap with some analyst/designers or designer/programmers, and the phases often overlap, with design or coding starting before the previous phase is complete.

There are typically two important aspects to ad hoc projects:

1. Minimizing elapsed time to deliver the applications
2. Keeping the overall costs of the project down

In other words, these projects are supposed to be done quickly and cheaply—the classic quick-and-dirty project. In practice, many of these projects follow a modified version of the waterfall approach, but with much less formality and a lot less documentation.

These projects typically have a very visible project plan that is drawn up by the project manager, usually following the waterfall life cycle. Analysis and high-level design activities are similar to the waterfall activities, but the level of documentation is lower and there is much less verification. The key difference is that when features are assigned to developers, they take however long it takes, and there is very little the organization can do to predict when each feature will be complete enough to test.

How the costs are kept down while the schedule is reduced is well documented in "The Soul of a New Machine," by Tracy Kidder [Kidder, 1982]. The developers are made to feel special, are encouraged to put their heart and soul into the project, and are subjected to whatever motivational tricks are thought to work. Organizations that have been burned by late slippage on projects will also ensure that work chunks given to the developers are relatively small, say two or three days of work, to ensure that progress toward eventual completion can be closely tracked.

Some organizations that have been burned by excessive defects from this approach with cowboy coders debugging their way to a running program have addressed this fear by having extensive testing programs. Some even go as far as to have alpha/beta releases to users who are willing to test the software for them.

The ad hoc approach can be successful with small projects when the development team has enough experience and enthusiasm. This is especially true when the project manager has worked with the team before. Running an ad hoc project allows the team to adjust their process to match the project. Unfortunately, in many cases, ad hoc projects run into trouble because it is very hard to achieve low cost and a short schedule simultaneously without paying a lot of attention to the management of the project.

Game Development

Although game development is often thought of as the prototypical last refuge of the cowboy coder, the reality is quite different. The game development community is actually quite active in trying to understand and refine their craft. Indeed, books have been written about game architecture [Rollings, 1999] and Web sites have been dedicated to "The Art and Science of Making Games" [http://www.gamasutra.com/]. The Gamasutra site even publishes postmortems from projects so that the game development community can learn from other projects.

Overall, although there is not one well-defined process that is accepted by the game development community, there is a common theme running through many game development projects. The important thing about most game development projects is deceptively simple: *predictable delivery of a stable product.*

For the vast majority of games, rapid delivery is not important. What matters is that the completion date can be predicted accurately so that marketing can build up demand for the game just prior to release. Building up momentum for the game is pointless if the game is not ready on time, and being early means that the team missed opportunities to add extra features and capabilities.

Unified Process Projects

The Unified Process is the de facto standard for modern software engineering projects. It supports incremental development in the context of a phased approach that enables projects to be planned, tracked, and compared. The Unified Process considers the following to be important:

- ◇ Designing the correct software architecture
- ◇ Making accurate estimates through detailed plans
- ◇ Providing traceability through documentation

The Unified Process uses a phased approach to make it easy to see the status of a project, but the phases are organized completely differently from a waterfall project. The first phase is *inception*, which is aimed at evaluating the economic feasibility of the project, forcing the team to define the overall project scope, plan the remaining phases, and produce estimates.

The next phase, *elaboration*, is aimed at evaluating the technical feasibility of the project. This requires the team to create and validate the overall software architecture by actually delivering a small subset of the functionality to test all the technology from end to end. The actual effort numbers from this phase are also used to refine and update the plans, estimates, and economic justification for the project.

The problem of changing requirements is dealt with during the *construction* phase by delivering incrementally. At the end of each increment, new and changed requirements can be incorporated into the plans, and the estimates can be refined based on experiences in the previous increments.

Traceability is important in the Unified Process because it addresses the large software engineering projects that used to employ the waterfall process. The documentation is needed to support the large teams but also to ensure that when a project is complete, there is an audit trail of all of the decisions that were made.

Although the Unified Process does not consider efficiency to be of primary importance, it does use analysis and domain models to ensure that design starts only when the requirements are well understood. Design models are also created and validated prior to programming so that the need to rework code once it is written is minimized.

Because the Unified Process is really a process framework, there have been attempts to tailor the framework for smaller team projects. To date, there is insufficient data to suggest whether this tailoring has been successful.

What Do Open Source Projects Consider Important?

This category is harder to categorize because, although there are good definitions for Open Source and Free Software Foundation GNU projects, the approach they use to software development varies.

Cathedral/Bazaar

Open Source–style projects are interesting because they are noncommercial, community projects. The original Free Software Foundation approach is explained in the GNU Manifesto [`http://www.fsf.org/gnu/manifesto.html`], which has been expanded into an overall philosophy for free software [`http://www.fsf.org/philosophy/philosophy.html`]. Although the Free Software Foundation was founded to create noncommercial alternatives to proprietary software, the Open Source Initiative [`http://www.opensource.org/`] seeks to apply a similar community development process but is not hostile to the idea of proprietary software.

Eric Raymond [Raymond, 1999] noticed that some projects are centrally directed (Cathedral-style projects), whereas some are built around a community of developers (Bazaar-style projects). The real difference between these styles is that the Bazaar style addresses what Richard Gabriel calls the problem of selection:

> *Great art is a process of making lots of things, knowing how to select the good ones, and knowing how to perfect them—making stuff, choosing critically, making some mistakes, being able to recognize them, and then being able to correct them.*
>
> *. . . the software creation discipline hasn't gotten to the selection part yet—each methodology I've described operates under the assumption that someone can know what to build and that by either thinking hard or making small, incremental modifications, we can build the right thing. No other practice of art demonstrates the truth of this proposition. We can build OK things, but not great things. In only a small number of cases have we made a diversity of software and then selected, and in most of those cases—such as for text editors—the ones we selected were not the best. [Gabriel, 2001]*

Linux is probably the prototypical Bazaar-style project that handles the selection process reasonably well. Any developer can contribute to the project by submitting code or bug fixes to one of the maintainers. The maintainers can then select the best version of the code or bug fix to include in the maintained sources. Open Source projects are not resource constrained. Many different solutions can be created and then the most appropriate one selected. Using Linux as an example is instructive because the selection and incorporation of available patches is not always smooth. Sometimes the maintainers disagree over which patches should be included, and sometimes useful patches are overlooked. Overall, though, it has proved to be an effective way of involving a large development community in the evolution of a software product.

The Open Source community considers the following to be important:

◈ Free, unrestricted access to the source code so that developers can share and learn
◈ The reputation of the project's developers
◈ Frequent releases back to the community

The frequent releases are very important because they demonstrate that the project is alive and they reward the contributors, who can see how their work has contributed to the whole.

Overall, the Open Source approach can be very successful if a large developer community gets behind the project. On the other hand, there are very many projects that just do not manage to attract enough developers for the project to take off [Raymond, 1999; Pavlicek, 2000].

Ruby Community

The Ruby programming language [http://www.ruby-lang.org/] is an example of a smaller Open Source project that highlights many of the issues surrounding Open Source style development. As a programming language project, it attracts a wide range of developers—from people interested in the design of programming languages, to developers wanting a better language in which to write programs, to educators looking for a new teaching language. Like many Open Source projects, it is still maintained by its originator, Yukihiro "Matz" Matsumoto, and although there is vigorous debate in the community about new and changed features, Matz retains absolute control over what he will accept into the core of Ruby. Overall, the issues that are important in the Ruby community are

◈ Maintaining a coherent vision in the face of competing needs
◈ Avoiding duplication of work
◈ Building on each other's contributions

Maintaining the vision is very important in the Ruby community and is expressed in the "Principle of Least Surprise," which features strongly in debates about language features. The idea is that the language should work the way that we expect it to work; it should not surprise us.

Duplication of work is avoided by having a central archive of modules and libraries that can be browsed through. The Ruby Application Archive [http://www.ruby-lang.org/en/raa.html] shows the status of all projects and provides contact details for the various authors. In addition, projects are announced and discussed on the Ruby e-mail lists and Usenet groups so the chances of unintentional duplication of work are minimized.

What Is Important to Agile Projects?

This category includes most of the approaches that led to the formation of the Agile Alliance [www.agilealliance.org]. Although there is a lot of common ground between these approaches as expressed in the Manifesto for Agile Software Development, the approaches turn out to be surprisingly diverse.

Manifesto for Agile Software Development

We are uncovering better ways of developing
software by doing it and helping others do it.
Through this work we have come to value:

Individuals and interactions over processes and tools
Working software over comprehensive documentation
Customer collaboration over contract negotiation
Responding to change over following a plan

That is, while there is value in the items on
the right, we value the items on the left more.

Kent Beck	James Grenning	Robert C. Martin
Mike Beedle	Jim Highsmith	Steve Mellor
Arie van Bennekum	Andrew Hunt	Ken Schwaber
Alistair Cockburn	Ron Jeffries	Jeff Sutherland
Ward Cunningham	Jon Kern	Dave Thomas
Martin Fowler	Brian Marick	

(© 2001, The above authors. This declaration may be freely copied in any form, but only in its entirety through this notice [http://www.agilemanifesto.org].)

- -

Generically, though, the Agile methods deal with the twin problems of haste and partial knowledge by using incremental development and by encouraging communication and learning within the team. Most Agile methods use development cycles of one month or less, which enables the team to learn rapidly how effective their process is at converting requirements into working software. This neatly addresses the problem of haste because there is regular feedback about the pace and effectiveness of the process that the team is using.

The Agile methods use diverse approaches to encouraging communication and learning, but all recognize the value of face-to-face communication. Some go as far as to insist on colocated teams; others just recognize that if the team is not colocated, then the team is going to have to expend more energy on sharing knowledge and disseminating information.

A defining characteristic of Agile methods is the way that they use rapid feedback to address the problems of haste and partial knowledge.

Adaptive Software Development

Adaptive Software Development is a collaborative approach to high-speed, high-change "extreme" projects. It provides a framework for managing projects in the face of partial knowledge in which the applications are needed quickly and the business faces competitive pressure to adapt and change rapidly. Adaptive Software Development considers the following to be important:

- Responding to uncertainty and emergence
- Choosing an appropriate mission profile
- Trusting people to do the right thing

Adaptive Software Development is designed to tackle the hard software development projects that require us to "challenge our most fundamental assumptions about software development." [Highsmith, 2000, p. 13] This approach addresses the issues of partial knowledge by acknowledging that "The greatest risk we face in software development is that of overestimating our own knowledge." [Highsmith, 2000, p. 13]

Choosing an appropriate mission profile is important because it is impossible for a project to excel in many dimensions simultaneously. Rather than strive for the impossible, Highsmith recommends that teams choose their priorities early and then make the appropriate tradeoffs so that the project is managed in a way that enables the team to create the desired outcome.

Adaptive Software Development is relatively unique among methodologies in that it is primarily focused on the importance of leadership, learning, and culture in achieving project success. Indeed, the entire focus is really on management and collaboration rather than on specific software development techniques.

Adaptive Software Development is very closely aligned to the principles expressed in the Manifesto for Agile Software Development. It differs from Extreme Programming in that it has very little to say about what the developer should actually do in the way of development techniques and practices. Instead, it sets up an environment that allows the team to focus on the project and then monitors the *workstate* rather than the workflow. It views rigor as a balancing force, not as a goal in and of itself.

Overall, Adaptive Software Development seems to accept and embrace the need for speed, but balances this with a project cycle that enables it to manage the resulting uncertainty. It uses a Speculate— Collaborate—Learn cycle to enable the team to proceed quickly while tackling the problems of partial knowledge [Highsmith, 2000].

Crystal

The Crystal methodologies are a related set of approaches to projects tailored for different-size teams and are optimized for different outcomes. They are a direct application of the idea that all processes are situational, and provide base guidelines for projects with different circumstances. Overall, Crystal considers the following to be important:

⬦ Trusting people to be good citizens
⬦ Using incremental development so the team gets practice at delivering
⬦ Being barely sufficient to avoid overloading people with process

Crystal addresses the twin problems of haste and partial knowledge by setting up an environment that encourages communication within the team and by using incremental development. Crystal acknowledges that different team sizes will need different communication strategies to allow for the fact that face-to-face communication, although effective in small teams, does not work as well with larger teams.

The idea of a barely sufficient methodology runs through Crystal. It is important to trust the team members to do the right thing rather than burden them with extra processes that may be inappropriate for the specific project. The reasoning behind this is that no matter how carefully the process documentation is written, the people on the team will do their own version of what was asked of them. Crystal is therefore very "sloppy" and tolerant of individual variations, trusting that with incremental development the team members will learn how to adjust their process to be successful.

The Crystal methodologies are very closely aligned with the Manifesto for Agile Software Development. The emphasis on communication and collaborative development is clearly evident [Cockburn, 1997, 2002].

Dynamic Systems Development Method

DSDM is an updated version of Rapid Application Development that pays attention to controlling and managing the rapid delivery of applications. It employs active user involvement and empowered teams to deliver quality applications through the use of "timeboxed" development. Overall, DSDM considers the following to be important:

- ✧ Doing enough and no more
- ✧ Promoting active user involvement to ensure fitness for business purpose
- ✧ Using iterative development to converge on an accurate solution

DSDM addresses the twin problems of haste and partial knowledge by using timeboxes to focus attention on delivering value. Iterative development within each timebox ensures that the design evolves to meet the needs of the users, while regression testing is used to ensure that the changes do not break existing code.

A secondary aspect to DSDM is that it takes care to ensure that projects are assessed for their suitability for DSDM before the project starts. The DSDM suitability filter is an essential part of DSDM in that it ensures that the method is not used on inappropriate projects. After all, the philosophy of doing enough and no more is great when a project is really pressed for time; however, when there is enough time, users will expect more functionality and features.

The timeboxing in DSDM is rigorous, with each timebox assigned some "must have," "should have," and "could have" features. "It is very important that not all things to be done in the timebox are 'must haves.' If they are, the content of the timebox should be revisited." [Stapleton, 1997, p. 31] The focus is on building a plan that gives all of the "must have" functionality by the agreed-on date. Anything else is a pure bonus that can be left out and delivered after the first release.

The fit between DSDM and the Manifesto for Agile Software Development is quite good. There is a strong focus on collaboration and empowered teams, but there is also a lot of emphasis on delivering to the agreed-on plan. DSDM pays a lot of attention to determining when an application is needed and then delivering on that date. Yes, there is flexibility about just what features the client requires by that date, but meeting the planned date is important.

Feature-Driven Development

Feature-Driven Development is a model-driven, short iteration process that is focused on delivering client-valued functionality every two weeks. Unlike most of the other Agile approaches, it is model driven and places a much higher value on modeling the problem domain (often through the use of CASE tools) than the other methods. Overall, Feature-Driven Development considers the following to be important:

✧ Frequent, tangible working results
✧ Precision tracking of progress
✧ Verification of all deliverables through clear process exit criteria

Feature-Driven Development addresses the twin problems of haste and partial knowledge by closely tracking progress through a two-week delivery cycle. Using a CASE tool and a model-driven process assists with rapid delivery, whereas delivering client-valued functionality every two weeks ensures that the team can quickly learn about what the client really needs.

One unique aspect of Feature-Driven Development is its use of a *Chief Programmer concept* that is close to the *Surgical Team* described in *The Mythical Man-Month*. [Brooks, 1995, p. 29] Features are assigned to a chief programmer who then forms a temporary *feature team* for the iteration. One of the key responsibilities of chief programmers is the mentoring of the members of their team.

The fit between Feature-Driven Development and the Manifesto for Agile Software Development is quite good. It is designed to deliver working software every two weeks, and allows the customer to choose the features to be delivered at every increment. On the other hand, it does place a high value on CASE tools, and the chief programmers are definitely in charge of the development process. Yes, it does consider individuals and their interactions important, it is just that the chief programmers count more than the other members of the development team [Coad, 1999].

Pragmatic Programming

Although *The Pragmatic Programmer* [Hunt, 2000] is not a traditional methodology book, both of the authors are signatories to the Manifesto for Agile Software Development. Unlike the other Agile approaches, Pragmatic Programming tackles the problems faced by teams of two or three developers. Overall, Pragmatic Programming considers the following to be important:

- Individual craftsmanship as a foundation for team success
- Effective, appropriate use of tools
- Continuous learning and improvement

Pragmatic Programming addresses the twin problems of haste and partial knowledge by encouraging learning and communication. By encouraging all developers to sign their work, it ensures that pride in work guards against unwise haste. At the same time, it encourages developers to automate whenever possible, and to learn how to use their tools so that they can become much more effective, efficient developers.

Pragmatic Programming guards against partial knowledge by viewing "requirements gathering, design and implementation as different facets of the same process—the delivery of a quality system." [Hunt, 2000, p. 218] It then goes on to say ". . . try to adopt a seamless approach: specification and implementation are simply different aspects of the same process—an attempt to capture and codify a requirement. Each should flow directly into the next, with no artificial boundaries. You'll find that a healthy development process encourages feedback from implementation and testing into the specification process." [Hunt, 2000, p. 218]

One interesting aspect of Pragmatic Programming is that it has zero tolerance for sloppy, obviously broken things—the "Don't Live with

Broken Windows" idea that it is easier to fight software entropy if everything is always kept immaculate [Hunt, 2000, p. 5].

The fit between Pragmatic Programming and the Manifesto for Agile Software Development is quite good. Pragmatic Programming pays a lot of attention to the individual developer and how they interact with the overall team. There is, however, a very strong focus on developers really taking the time to learn and become comfortable with their development tools. Developers are also encouraged to be continually questioning, striving to understand and improve their own process. Overall, the lasting impression is that the Pragmatic Programming approach is very similar to XP in that it deals with what the developers should do, and is confident that it can deliver anything that the customer could reasonably ask for.

Scrum

Scrum is a very interesting approach to software product development that is being successfully applied to other types of software projects. Interestingly, it is more a technique for managing skilled developers than it is a software development methodology. It says very little about how the developers should do their work, but says a lot about how management should interact with and guide the development team. Overall, Scrum considers the following to be important:

◇ Allowing the team to focus on delivering value
◇ Demonstrating the functionality to all stakeholders
◇ Managing empirically through firsthand information

Scrum addresses the twin problems of haste and partial knowledge by structuring the project team to allow the developers to focus on the task at hand. It divides a project into a series of "sprints," within which the team agrees to deliver on the spirit of the "Sprint Goal"—an agreed-on amount of demonstrable functionality. Within each sprint, the team is allowed to focus on the tasks at hand, with management ensuring that external distractions have minimal impact on the team. Scrum changes the relationship between developers and managers by casting managers in the role of resources for the team, with daily Scrum meetings that enable the team to inform the managers of any impediments to progress. Removing these impediments to progress is a key management responsibility in Scrum.

The fit between Scrum and the Manifesto for Agile Software Development is very good. The team is empowered, demonstrations of working software happen at the end of each sprint, the customers are closely involved, and at the end of each sprint, the plans are adjusted to match the current reality [Schwaber, 2002].

Summary

   ✧ All too many projects do little if any risk management or risk mitigation, so it does not seem that many projects are managed as if the basic problem is risk.

   ✧ Few traditional methodologies pay enough attention to testing and quality assurance. The right words are said, but when the crunch comes, quality assurance is seen as an optional part of the process.

   ✧ Most traditional processes assume that the cost of rework is high. Agile processes assume that rework is a natural part of the development process. As the team learns, rework allows the new knowledge to improve the software.

   ✧ Agile methods deal with the twin problems of haste and partial knowledge by using incremental development and by encouraging communication and learning within the team.

   ✧ A defining characteristic of Agile methods is the way that they use rapid feedback to address the problems of haste and partial knowledge.

   ✧ All of the Agile methods have their own unique interpretation of what it means to be aligned with the Manifesto for Agile Software Development.

Chapter 5

What Is Important for Your Projects?

Some days I like to imagine what life would be like without computers or software.

Given your history and experiences with projects, you will have your own set of concerns and worries about projects. The rest of the people in your organization have their own experiences and backgrounds that will lead them to have their own concerns and worries. All of this makes it a challenging task to compare and evaluate the various approaches to software development.

Selecting the most appropriate approach would be difficult if the field of software development was relatively static, but it is not. It is practically a cliché to say that software development is a rapidly changing field. So rather than attempt the impossible, maybe you should settle for finding a workable approach that is acceptable to your organization.

Reinterpreting Experience in the Light of New Knowledge

Reinterpreting your experiences is very important in times of change. The reason is that as things change, we need to see if what we learned in the past is still applicable and relevant. An example of this is the difficulty of reading source code to understand what a program is supposed to do. Historically, this has been really hard to do in assembler and low-level languages, so the lesson we learned was that programs need lots of external documentation and that printed diagrams are really useful for understanding the structure of a program. With modern, expressive object-oriented programming languages, it might be time to reevaluate how much external documentation is needed to make the code understandable. Similarly, with a good development environment, maybe diagrams can be generated from the source code on the fly, so the need for diagrams to show the original design might go away.

A more appropriate example is possibly the assertion by the Extreme Programming community that the cost-of-change curve is no longer exponential. Although it is probably not flat, it is still useful to question the "get it right the first time" lesson we learned from the exponential curve. It may also be useful to ask what would it take to flatten the curve even further. Also, in the light of the effectiveness of incremental methods, maybe the whole concept of "get it right the first time" is obsolete, and what we now need is a "fast failure." By getting something out quickly, the users will be able to guide the development team to an appropriate solution.

My challenge to you is to identify other things that you know that are possibly suspect in light of all of the changes that have happened in software development over the years. Maybe it is time you reconsidered some of your own knowledge and expertise.

Understanding Process, Culture, and Methodologies

One thing you should be wary of is claims made by methodologists. As Alistair Cockburn has pointed out [Cockburn 2002], methodologies are notoriously hard to get right and to tune. A tried-once methodology is likely to be harmful to your peace of mind. Even if a process has been used successfully many times, it does not mean that your team will be able to replicate those successes.

You should never underestimate the difficulty of changing to a different approach to developing software. Adopting and adjusting a methodology to fit your organization and projects will take considerable calendar time and is likely to be accompanied by an initial drop in productivity. The people in your organization need to retrain their reflexes to match the expectations of the new approach, and because this will typically involve espousing and acting on new values, you cannot expect it to happen overnight. Changing organizational cultures is an intriguing subject for study, but rarely something that you want to tackle just to get slightly better software development. In most cases you need to choose an approach that fits the organization's culture.

- -

Probably the best thing that can happen to an organization from the point of view of making it easy to switch to a different approach is to have a complete and utter disaster of a project. In the aftermath of that kind of project there is normally space for a new approach to be adopted and welcomed.

Ideally, you also want the disaster to be of sufficient magnitude that the only really useful artifact from the previous project is the extra knowledge in the heads of the team members about the problem domain. It is much easier to put a new approach in place at the start of a project than to retrofit a new approach into an ongoing project.

Indeed, this is a major challenge when changing approaches. Most methodologies assume that they are going to be used in a "green-field" project, whereas in reality most projects are extensions and additions to existing applications. There is very little written down about how to switch from one approach to another in the middle of a project.

Be very scared of approaches that suggest you should throw away your existing code and start over again with the new approach. Although this sometimes is touted as the only way to rescue a failing project, it is also a really good way to mess up. Even though the idea that we should "plan to throw one away" was enshrined as good advice by Fred Brooks [Brooks, 1995, p. 115], times have changed and it is rarely the best strategy any more.

Indeed, Joel Spolsky has called this one of the "things you should never do" [Spolsky, 2000] when writing about the decision by Netscape to completely rewrite its browser. The problem is that the source code represents a massive investment of time, energy, and knowledge about the application. Starting again from scratch is expensive, and there is no guarantee that it will be any better the second time. In practical terms it is nearly always better to try to fix up the existing code than it is to start over, but few methodologists offer advice about improving existing code. If you are in this situation, you need to check out a book called *Refactoring* [Fowler, 1999].

Maintenance and Evolution of the Software

When comparing approaches, be wary of approaches that do not say much about maintenance and evolution of software. Practically everyone involved in software development has had the experience of releasing a new application and then finding themselves inundated with requests for enhancements and tweaks.

Some people claim that this just shows that the project team didn't spend enough time analyzing and trying to understand the real user requirements. Others claim that there is an emergence effect. Each new application or feature changes the users' environment and, through interacting in that changed environment, users will discover new opportunities and needs. Every approach to software development should have a strategy for emergent requirements because the newly emerged opportunities may be even more valuable than the original application.

My personal view is that although emergence is real, few projects really take the time to explore the requirements space as well as they could [Gause, 1989]. By applying some creative thinking, many projects would face fewer late-breaking surprises. The challenge for projects is to balance exploratory thinking against the need to deliver the software in a short period of time. Many projects deliver less imme-diate value than they could by spending too much effort thinking about what could be, rather than delivering what is currently wanted and needed. Either way, all projects are faced with the need to deliver enhancements, whether immediately or in a year or two as neighboring applications change and evolve.

Anecdotal evidence suggests that more is spent on software mainte-nance and evolution than is spent on the project that created the initial version. So although an approach that deals with new projects is impor-tant, it is probably more important to have an approach that protects this initial investment. You could try to have one approach for new projects and another for maintenance, but that brings us to the topic of the next section. Can multiple approaches really work in one organization?

Can a Methodology per Project Really Work?

Although many methodologists would agree with Alistair Cockburn when he states that we need a "Methodology per project," it is, as he states, the *wrong answer* from an organizational standpoint [Cockburn, 2002, p. 141].

It is a wrong answer because organizations want a simple answer. They do not want to have to tailor their process to every project. What the organization wants is an inexpensive means of doing project oversight, and typically this means having a mechanism to compare projects over time. It is much harder to compare projects if they are using different approaches. After all, who can tell if a waterfall project that has just completed the design phase is ahead or behind compared with a Unified Process project that has just completed the elaboration phase?

Yes, a one-off process is OK for a special, high-importance, skunkworks project because the organization can afford to spend more on monitoring one special project. The rest of the projects get managed on an exception basis, where the project gets looked at closely only if it stands out from the rest. For this to happen, the approaches used on the projects must all have similar reporting mechanisms so that projects are directly comparable.

So What Is Important to Your Projects?

Although you are the only person who can really answer this question, my aim in this section is to suggest areas to which your software development approach should pay attention. Whatever approach you choose, you need to make sure that it fits with your organization and the people working on the projects. It is important that your key people are willing to use the new approach. Your new approach has to be acceptable to the bulk of your staff because you cannot afford to alienate or lose them.

Another important item for you to discover is whether switching to a new approach will give sufficient return on investment to make the switch worthwhile. When working this out, you need to factor in the costs of switching existing projects and applications. For most organizations, the cost of switching to a different approach will dramatically outweigh the benefits unless the organization is obviously suffering from failing projects.

You should try to determine whether a new approach will enable projects to give a good return on investment. The key here is that the projects deliver and the resulting applications can evolve and can be maintained economically for the rest of their planned life. Obviously delivery matters, but for the long-term health of the organization, the delivered applications must have a long, useful life. After all, most organizations cannot afford to replace core systems very often.

You will also need to find an approach that fits with the culture and values expressed by your organization. An exploratory approach is inefficient in an optimizing organization, just as an optimizing approach is too rigid for an exploratory organization [Highsmith, 2000].

The key questions, however, are the ones that only you can answer:

- ✧ Is your current approach to software development broken?
- ✧ Are your projects really time constrained? Is the business willing to accept less functionality to get an earlier delivery?
- ✧ Are your projects functionality constrained? Is the business willing to wait until all the functionality is ready?
- ✧ Are your projects life or safety critical? Are there any regulatory agencies that have to approve any process change?
- ✧ Are your users able to contribute significant time to steer and guide your projects?
- ✧ Are your projects redefining your overall business processes? Are you stepping into uncharted territory?
- ✧ Do your projects use bleeding-edge technology? Do your projects rely on technological innovation to be successful?
- ✧ Are your lead developers enthusiastic about using the new Agile approach?
- ✧ Are your project managers enthusiastic about using the new Agile approach?
- ✧ Are your users comfortable with the idea of working with partial knowledge?
- ✧ Are your users comfortable with the idea of emergent requirements, or could the team get blamed for not getting it right the first time?
- ✧ Are your projects valuable enough that the disruption of moving to a new approach is worth the potential benefits?
- ✧ Does your organization have the stamina to stay the course of switching to a new process? Or is it forever seeking a silver bullet?

At this point you will probably find it useful to look back over the previous two chapters to see how appropriate the various approaches are, given what you know about your organization.

Learning From XP to Improve Your Process

If, however, all you need is process improvement, then it may not be appropriate to look at switching approaches. What you need to do in this case is question Extreme Programming to see what lessons can be learned and whether there are any practices that can be borrowed to improve your current approach. Although this will mean that your team members cannot wear the "We are doing XP" T-shirt, it will allow them to improve their delivery of applications, which is (after all) the whole point of the exercise.

Summary

- As things change we need to see if what we learned in the past is still applicable and relevant.
- Be very wary of claims made by methodologists.
- A tried-once methodology is likely to be harmful to your peace of mind.
- Never underestimate the difficulty of changing to a different software development process.
- There is very little information about how to switch from one approach to another in the middle of a project.
- Be wary of approaches that do not say much about maintenance and evolution of software.
- A "methodology per project" is the *wrong answer* from an organizational standpoint.
- If your current approach to software development is not broken, it is unlikely that you can recoup the cost of changing to a different process.

Part III

Questioning the Core XP Practices

Keep practicing. There is no shortcut to mastery.

Having looked at the fears that drive the various approaches, we have to ask this question: How well do the Extreme Programming practices address these fears? Initially, the question will relate to the fears that motivate Extreme Programming, but the last chapter of this section will probe deeper and ask questions related to the wider issues addressed by other approaches.

This section is organized into five chapters that focus on different aspects of software development:

1. "Planning Incremental Development" looks at how XP projects are planned and the implications this has for everyone involved in the project.
2. "Truly Incremental Development" looks at what it means to work on a project in which everything is constrained to fit within small time boxes.
3. "Are We Done Yet?" looks a how crucial issues around quality are addressed in XP projects.
4. "Working at This Intensity Is Hard" looks at the people issues surrounding XP projects.
5. "Is That All There Is to Extreme Programming?" wraps up this section by looking at what is missing from XP compared with other approaches.

These practices are intended to be used within the context of the XP project lifecycle [Beck, 2000, p. 131–137]. Lifecycle phases are no longer really emphasized in Extreme Programming because the overall goal, as Kent Beck stated when reviewing an early draft of this book (personal communication, January 2000), is "to create a completely self-similar process, where you are doing essentially the same activities at all timescales from minutes to decades and day 1 to day 10,000." It is, however, instructive to see how these phases differ from the phases in traditional projects:

◇ **Exploration**—This is a short phase during which the team experiments with the technology to gain confidence in estimating the stories that are being created by the customer.

◇ **Planning**—This is a very short phase during which the team creates the initial release plan that shows the date by which the "smallest, most valuable set of stories will be done."

◇ **Iterations to First Release**—During this phase the team works in short iterations to deliver tested functionality. Every three or four iterations, the release plan is updated to reflect the performance of the team and changes to the requirements.

◇ **Productionizing**—This phase is the end game of the initial iterations, leading up to the first release of the software to live production use.

◇ **Maintenance**—This phase is the normal state of an XP project. At the end of each iteration, the new and changed features are ready for release to production use.

◇ **Death (of the project)**—When the customer cannot think of any more useful features, the team writes the documentation that will be needed for future enhancements and modifications, and the team is then disbanded, leaving the software in live production.

Of all of these phases, Maintenance is the one that is expected to last the longest. It starts when the first release goes live and continues as long as the customer can think of valuable features that need to be added to the application. The team activities during this phase make up the core practices of XP.

Chapter 6

Planning Incremental
Development

Everyone develops incrementally; the difference is in the size of the increments.

The planning practices are based on the idea of minimizing the risk of schedule slippage while maximizing the opportunity for the users to verify that their needs have been understood and the business has not changed. Extreme Programming differs from many other approaches because it focuses on delivering the "smallest, most valuable set of stories" [Beck, 2000, p. 133]. By utilizing very short iterations, XP eliminates the possibility of large, unexpected schedule slips, and by delivering working software every few weeks, XP provides direct feedback about the quality of the estimates to reduce the chance of even small, unexpected slips.

The XP approach to planning follows the *Evolutionary Delivery* approach advocated by Tom Gilb in *Principles of Software Engineering Management* [Gilb, 1988, p. 83–113]. The basic idea is to get something valuable into production as soon as possible. This addresses the fears about the project slipping or getting canceled, reduces the risk that the business will change, and provides an early checkpoint that the business has not been misunderstood.

Small Releases

Understanding the fears that drive Extreme Programming is key to understanding the practice of *small releases*. Programmers are scared of delivering the wrong thing and of delivering late. By delivering a small but very valuable chunk of functionality in a short period of time, the development team mitigates both of these risks. In XP, the *Release Plan* shows the functionality that will be in each of these small releases. Each release is made up of a number of iterations, each of which has an *Iteration Plan* detailing the work for that iteration. The Release Plan is created during the *Planning Game*, whereas the Iteration Plan is recreated at the start of each iteration.

Estimating is much easier when there is only a small amount of work to estimate. It is much easier to predict how much work the team can do in the next two or three months than it is to predict how much work the team can do in a year. It is even easier when the supporting *User Stories* practice is added into the mix, because the team is building their estimate from small one- or two-week chunks of work.

User Stories

The risk of misunderstanding the business is mitigated by delivering the most valuable functionality first. *User Stories* help here as well, because they are small, discrete, testable units of functionality. The other thing that really helps to avoid misunderstandings is the somewhat counterintuitive factor that there is a lack of detail in the written user stories. This helps because it means that the programmer has to talk to the users (the *On-site Customer*) to find out what exactly is required. The daily conversations that occur while the users explain what exactly is meant by the user story means that a misunderstanding is not likely to go unnoticed, especially because this is a feature that the user considers valuable.

User stories are primarily intended to identify the requirements so that the project team members remember to have conversations about them. The programmers work from what the users say, not from a written requirements specification. This mitigates the risk that the requirements documentation is out of date, because the On-site Customer is assumed to know what is needed.

Planning Game

The *Planning Game* is used to allocate user stories to iterations and releases. The planning game has a well-defined set of moves that, in essence, state that the business gets to specify the functionality (user stories), the relative priorities of each story, and the ideal release dates. The developers get to estimate the work content of each story and hence the number of stories that can be completed during each iteration. Based on this information, the business can then choose a release date based on the functionality they need in the next release. The Release Plan is an overall project plan that the business can use for overall estimating and budgeting purposes, and for determining when the value of extra functionality is outweighed by the additional development costs.

Developing in short two- or three-week iterations imposes a discipline on the programming team and gives the business regular confirmation that it has not been misunderstood. At the end of each iteration, all the user stories allocated to that iteration are supposed to be 100 percent complete and tested. The On-site Customer can look at the test results and see the new features in the application to confirm whether the user stories have been successfully and correctly implemented. Misunderstandings are easy to detect, as are mismatches between the feature as requested and changes to the business process (which are unlikely to occur in the three weeks from when the story was first explained to when the completed functionality was delivered).

Small releases are still necessary, however, because there is always the possibility that the On-site Customer has missed something. By putting small releases into live production, the value of the new features is demonstrated. By releasing to live production use, two other fears are addressed: defect rate and false feature rich. When new features go live, the user community will be very vocal if there are any defects or cool but useless features have delayed any requested features.

One added benefit of working in iterations toward a small release is that the developers get lots of practice in estimating and delivering on those estimates. This means that it is very easy for the organization to determine whether the release plan is viable. If each iteration has to defer some user stories to the next iteration, the next release date is going to be missed unless some functionality is dropped. No more big, last-minute surprises—the organization can confirm the validity of the release plan at the end of each iteration.

After each small release, the new production software becomes the foundation for the next set of iterations, building toward the next small release.

Open Questions

Although these practices seem to address the fears that XP has, and the mutual synergy of these practices seems to make sense, there are many open questions.

From my personal background in using Use Cases to identify and capture requirements, I suspect there are some complex domains in which the On-site Customer might not have the necessary domain knowledge to be able to answer all the programmer's questions in a timely manner. Alistair Cockburn has some anecdotal evidence from one project [Cockburn, 2002] in which the business analysts needed lots of supporting documentation behind each user story.

There is also the question regarding whether the requirements can be split up into small enough chunks to be delivered in a single iteration. Because user stories have to be small (ideally, less than three developer weeks of work) it remains to be seen whether this can be done for all projects.

The accuracy of the estimates produced during the planning game needs to be investigated, especially for organizations that are just adopting XP. Although an experienced XP team with an experienced customer might be able to make good predictions about schedule and feature content, I doubt the same could be said for teams that are just adopting XP. Yes, there is a lot written about planning in XP [Beck and Fowler, 2001], but I wonder how long it takes a new XP team to get good at the Planning Game.

There is still a lot of controversy regarding whether it is really possible to do small releases for all types of projects. Tom Gilb maintained that it was always possible [Gilb, 1988, p. 243], but I consider this to be an open question. Kent Beck suggests that it is too risky to take more than six months for the initial release [Beck, 2000, p. 133]. The problem from an XP standpoint is that there will be too much investment without feedback from actual, live usage of the system. The twin risks of defect rate or false feature rich could mean that the project will be a failure when it eventually goes live.

Success with the planning game relies on a shift in organizational behavior so that the organization accepts the estimates given by the programmers. How likely is it that command and control-style organizations can successfully delegate responsibility for estimating down to the programmers? Many organizations seem to prefer the idea of *stretch targets*—the idea that if the manager reduces the time available, the team will work harder to meet this new target. This attitude that people will slack off unless pushed is, however, fundamentally at odds with the XP Rights and Responsibilities [Jeffries, 2001, p. 7]:

> *"Programmer Rights #4 You have the right to make and update your own estimates."*

Imposed estimates are such an endemic problem in software development that I suspect that few organizations will be able to use the planning game successfully. To be successful with the planning game, an organization has to rearrange the overall responsibilities for planning and estimating. The customer is responsible for choosing the features, and the programmers who will do the work are responsible for creating the estimate by asking detailed questions about each feature.

Another open question is how easy it will be to fit XP into the standard project management framework that many organizations use. After all, the detailed assignment of people to tasks that is required on most PERT charts only happens within an iteration. The detailed tasks for each iteration are only planned at the start of the iteration, because deferring the selection of user stories until the start of each iteration allows the customer maximal freedom to steer the overall project.

What Can Other Approaches Learn From XP?

On the positive side, though, there is much that can be learned from the XP approach to planning. The practice of Small Releases has reintroduced and popularized Tom Gilb's ideas about *Evolutionary Delivery* [Gilb, 1988, p. 83] and, in the process, has restarted the conversation about the economics of software development [Baetjer, 1998]. Small Releases is a step beyond the ideas of *Spiral Development* as introduced by Barry Boehm [Boehm, 1981] because of the idea of getting the software ready for delivery at the end of each iteration.

A key idea behind XP planning is that a project should plan to get something useful into production as soon as possible. This is in marked contrast to many other Agile approaches, which focus on getting things into a reviewable state. In this, XP is repeating the advice given in Tom Gilb's "how little?" principle: "The ideal next evolutionary step costs as little as possible to implement, and gives as much as possible in the way of results to the end user." [Gilb, 1988, p. 101]

The economic argument is that by minimizing the investment required before the new features are operational, the return on the investment will be better, and less up-front investment is required. Another added advantage is that it is easier to estimate a smaller chunk of functionality than a larger chunk, and with frequent releases, the team soon learns how to improve the estimates.

Separating requirements identification and prioritization from the potentially much longer requirements capture and documentation activities is another useful lesson from XP that can be transferred to other approaches. Low-precision use cases [Cockburn, 2001] are sufficient for planning and prioritization purposes. The extra details and precision can be added when necessary just prior to the time that the developers need to start working on the use case.

The clear separation of roles and responsibilities in the Planning Game is also something that many other approaches could learn from. The software development community has always paid lip service to the idea that the person who is going to do the work is the person who should create the estimate. XP, however, is very vocal about the distinct roles involved in planning [Jeffries, 2001, p. 7].

The idea of developing inside, fixed-duration timeboxes is something that XP shares with most of the other Agile approaches. Timeboxes really help keep projects on track because they focus the attention of the entire team on meeting a ship date [McConnell, 1996, p. 575–583]. The team cannot easily delude itself into thinking that it will make up time later if every two or three weeks there is concrete proof of how much the team managed to deliver in one timebox.

Summary

- Extreme Programming differs from many other approaches because it focuses on delivering the "smallest, most valuable set of stories."
- The basic idea is to get something valuable into production as soon as possible.
- User stories are intended to identify the requirements so that the project team members remember to have conversations about them.
- Success with the planning game relies on a shift in organizational behavior so that the organization accepts the estimates given by the programmers.

Chapter 7

Truly Incremental Development

Is it a good idea to minimize the elapsed time taken to go from requirements elicitation to tested, running code?

The really extreme part of XP is the way it insists on incremental development. XP attempts to minimize the elapsed time from when a user describes some functionality in detail to when that functionality is ready for the user to test and use. The speed at which the team can turn a conversation about a feature into tested, running code is the cornerstone of XP. All the practices are geared toward making this as fast and reliable as possible.

XP is different because it does not use a phased approach to software development. Everything is done concurrently and incrementally. Requirements identification and capture, estimating, planning, design, coding, and testing are all done incrementally. This supports the planning strategy of working in short, timeboxed iterations by making it possible to deliver functionality quickly.

Simple Design

With an On-site Customer available to answer all requirements questions, Simple Design is the way that XP delivers incrementally. By insisting on "the simplest design that could possibly work," Simple Design forces the programmers to work continually on refining the design. As Kent Beck states:

The simplest design for the software at any given time is the one that

1. Runs all the tests.

2. Has no duplicated logic.

3. States every intention important to the programmers.

4. Has the fewest possible classes and methods. [Beck, 2000, p. 57]

Although these rules are very simple, they directly address many of the fears that motivate XP. Systems in which the code clearly expresses intention and there is no duplication of logic are easier to maintain and evolve, thus addressing the fears that the system will go sour or the defect rate will be too high.

Simple Design prevents applications from becoming *false feature rich* because the programmers have to remove any classes or methods that are not required to pass all of the tests. Simple Design states that the best design has the fewest possible classes and methods. This is the YAGNI rule—You Aren't Gonna Need It—in action. A feature can be added to the design only if there is a demonstrable, immediate need for it. This rule also helps address the risk of schedule slips, because rather than having to design in flexibility for future possible requirements, the programmers are required to create a simple design that supports the current functionality.

These rules also force a continual design activity because whenever duplicate logic is discovered, the programmers have to put on their Refactoring hat and remove the duplication.

Refactoring

The *Refactoring* practice addresses the biggest fear: that the system will become unmaintainable. Refactoring means "improving the design of existing code" [Fowler, 1999], and is central to preventing the system going sour. It is one of the key design activities in XP, the one that forces the developers to keep the code clean and the design simple on a daily basis.

Refactoring supports Simple Design by providing a checklist of known "code smells" [Fowler, 1999, p. 75] that indicate the design is not as simple as it could be. It is interesting to note, however, that the practice of Refactoring has to be supported by really strong and stringent Testing practices and Continuous Integration. Without these two, Refactoring would be exceedingly risky, error prone, and likely to slow down the overall speed of development.

System Metaphor

The *System Metaphor* is a practice that prevents the system from going sour. Strangely enough, it is another practice that is focused on design. The system metaphor for a project defines the architecture of the application and enables developers to talk about the aesthetics of the overall design. It is based on the earlier System of Names pattern documented by Ward Cunningham [Cunningham, 2001].

Interestingly, the System Metaphor also helps prevent business misunderstandings because the metaphor helps the On-site Customer understand the overall design. It also helps address the risk of staff turnover, because the existing design can be explained to a new team member using the system metaphor to direct the conversation. The system metaphor acts as a mnemonic device to allow the team members to remember the important design decisions.

Collective Code Ownership

The *Collective Code Ownership* practice targets multiple fears. It supports Simple Design by enabling anyone who sees a violation of the design rules to clean up the problem. It reduces the risk of schedule slips because a programmer never has to wait for someone else to make a change to some other class.

Collective Code Ownership is also a practice that enables large-scale Refactoring to improve the design. Without this, it would be impossible to coordinate changes when a widely used method is changed. It also promotes team cross-training, which protects against problems caused by staff turnover. Because everyone owns the code, the programmers are encouraged to look around and get familiar with all of the code, as opposed to the more usual practice of every developer jealously guarding their "own" code.

Continuous Integration

The last practice that is essential to truly incremental development is *Continuous Integration*. This practice mitigates the risk of last-minute surprises causing schedule slips because it ensures that there are never masses of changes to be integrated. It also keeps the defect rate down because, as part of integration, programmers must run the tests to ensure that their changes have not broken anything else.

Continuous Integration also reassures the business that everything is proceeding normally, because at every point through the project it is possible to build the application and demonstrate the functionality that has been built to date.

Interestingly, Continuous Integration also supports the programmer habits necessary for truly incremental development and Simple Design. Programmers are expected to work in short episodes of *Test First Design* and to integrate whenever they reach a convenient stopping point. To reinforce this, they are not allowed to "let the sun set on bad code," which effectively means that they have to integrate their changes by the end of the day or throw the code away and start afresh the next day.

Open Questions

The short-cycle, incremental development practices are probably the most controversial aspects of XP. After all, coding starts much too early without the team spending enough time doing analysis and design. The pressure to deliver something every two or three weeks means that design will never be able to happen. Everyone involved in software development has had trouble at one time or another with an undisciplined, unskilled developer who just sat down and started coding. In all probability, the developer managed to deliver something, but it was probably buggy, hard to extend, and nobody else could understand it. Once you have been burned by this type of undisciplined hacking, you never want to get burned again.

Although I can see parallels between undisciplined hacking and XP to the extent that it really values the coding activity, I think that developers have to be very disciplined to succeed with XP. If the developers forget to integrate their changes every day, defer Refactoring too long, drift away from the system metaphor, and do not practice Simple Design, the system could go sour really fast. So is a high level of discipline sustainable in the long run? Yes, teams successfully maintained the discipline for several years, but is it sustainable for 10 or 20 years? Can the discipline necessary for XP be achieved in teams that are used to more tolerant, relaxed approaches to software development?

The wide acceptability of Collective Code Ownership is also doubtful. In the past, some developers used to feel that someone else reading their program was an invasion of privacy, as if you were reading their personal diaries. Although this attitude is not as common these days, developers still take pride in what they have written, and getting used to the idea that others will change their work could be challenging for some.

Collective Code Ownership instills a sense of responsibility for the overall application, which can be very beneficial for the overall project but, at the same time, it diffuses individual accountability. With all the developers having their hands on the code, it is hard for an outside observer to assess the capabilities of the individual developers. Yes, it makes for better applications, but some organizations prefer to give raises and bonuses to individuals rather than rewarding the entire team. The counterargument to this, however, is that organizations who focus on individuals over teams should not really be attempting to adopt a collaborative development process like XP.

The idea that developers should strive for a Simple Design also runs counter to many tenets of programming culture. Indeed, there have been many Obfuscated C contests over the years [www.ioccc.org], in which the goal is to write the most obscure, obfuscated C program. It is easy to imagine contestants reading Roedy Green's essay on "How To Write Unmaintainable Code" [Green, 1997], but it is unlikely any of his suggestions would go down well on an XP project. Of course, even the contestants would admit that obfuscated code is not a good idea on a real project, and that they compete to write obfuscated code to demonstrate their mastery of the programming language. On the other hand, their mastery shows up in tight, well-written code that can look obfuscated to people with less knowledge of the programming language. Should they be forced to "dumb down" their code just because there are some members of the team who do not understand the programming language as well as they do?

Simple Design seems to discount the value that experienced developers can bring to the process. Many experienced developers prefer to put some investment into general infrastructure to give more flexibility than is strictly needed to meet the rules of Simple Design. Yes, the XP way prevents developers from adding unnecessary functionality, but some experienced developers think that XP goes too far in that it prevents them from judiciously applying their experience. After all, if you know you are going to have to refactor the code in a few days, why not start off with the refactored version, even if it is not strictly needed right now? If you know how it is going to have to be changed, why not write it that way now?

XP addresses its fears about unmaintainable code by turning software development into a maintenance task. The basic paradigm is that at all times there is a working application to which developers are continually adding enhancements. In every iteration, a new set of enhancements is requested, and the developers work with the On-site Customer to understand the new functionality and to make the necessary changes to the application.

From the viewpoint of people who learned to do thorough up-front analysis and design, this incremental approach is definitely an inefficient, questionable practice, possibly bordering on malpractice. Again, it comes down to fears. XP fears emergent requirements and unmaintainable code much more than it fears being accused of inefficiency. XP provides an opportunity every two or three weeks for new, emergent requirements to be identified and incorporated into the overall design as the customer steers each successive iteration. The massive distance between XP's incremental approach and the more traditional, up-front analysis and design leaves an open question regarding whether it is possible to reconcile these two opposing worldviews.

The System Metaphor practice has been criticized as one of the reasons that it is hard to apply XP in large teams:

> Metaphor is the least well defined of the XP practices. . . . Metaphor is insufficient as design, though, as its relationship to the solution is often rather loose. Indeed, as the team size grows, the ability for the metaphor to be sufficient decreases. [Crocker, 2001]

The question here is whether a System Metaphor is appropriate for generating a design, or is it more appropriate as a means of explaining and remembering a design? Yes, the System Metaphor is meant to be evocative, but this does not mean that that it will generate the design. More work still needs to be done on assisting XP teams in understanding how to do incremental design and how the use of a System Metaphor assists Refactoring.

What Can Other Approaches Learn From XP?

Many project teams have successfully managed to use the ideas behind Refactoring to improve the maintainability and readability of their code. In most cases it has been used to clean up code that the team "inherited" from another team or project.

Similarly, many teams practice a form of Continuous Integration, but there are still a lot of project teams that experience integration problems later on in the project because developers have been working too far away from the mainline code. Personally, I have been on projects on which a developer kept files checked out for more than eight weeks. I think that he was the only person on the team who was surprised by how hard it was to integrate his changed source code back into the main project.

Many projects could benefit from using a simpler architecture that is easier to explain and elaborate. In many cases a system goes sour because the project team does not really understand the overall architecture. The ideas behind System Metaphor could help here because they encourage the entire team to think about the application architecture.

There are also some useful lessons in Simple Design, but this goes against the grain for many developers who have been taught to value the potential for reuse. Some projects fail because they attempt to design components immediately for general, enterprisewide reuse before gaining experience on how the components are to be used in a single application. The resulting speculative generalization of the feature set often leads to bloated components that cannot be used effectively in any application. One lesson from this is that it is better to gain experience with using a component in one or more applications before attempting to make the component reusable.

Summary

- The really extreme part of XP is the way it insists on incremental development.
- The short-cycle, incremental development practices are probably the most controversial aspects of XP.
- Although I can see parallels between undisciplined hacking and XP to the extent that it really values the coding activity, I think that developers have to be very disciplined to succeed with XP.

- ✧ The idea that developers should strive for a Simple Design runs counter to many tenets of programming culture.

- ✧ Simple Design seems to discount the value that experienced developers can bring to the process.

- ✧ From the viewpoint of people who learned to do thorough up-front analysis and design, this incremental approach is definitely an inefficient, questionable practice, possibly bordering on malpractice.

- ✧ The massive distance between XP's incremental approach and the more traditional up-front analysis and design leaves an open question regarding whether it is possible to reconcile these two opposing worldviews.

Chapter 8

Are We Done Yet?

Software is never finished, but some of it is shipped.

As you might expect, XP has a unique viewpoint on testing as well as programming. Testing is meant to be a completely integral part of the development iterations. Teams that diligently and successfully do all of the XP practices should be able to take the application at the end of any iteration and give it to customers for live production use. No further parallel runs or customer tests should be needed. The On-site Customer should be confident that the software is ready for prime time.

XP is serious about fitting everything into the timeboxed iterations. If final acceptance testing happens outside (read, after) the iteration, the feedback about quality is delayed. It makes little sense for a team to say that it can add some necessary features during the next two- or three-week iteration if it will then take another month for the changed application to be tested.

Coding Standards

The *Coding Standards* address the fears about maintainability and enable the Collective Code Ownership and Refactoring practices. They are an essential part of XP because they define what well-written code looks like. As such, they complement the Simple Design practice and define the internal code quality to minimize the risk that the system will go sour.

Test First Development

Of all of the practices of XP, *Test First Development* is the most counterintuitive of them all. It is probably also the most powerful of them all for promoting the necessary paradigm shift for understanding and benefiting from Extreme Programming. The idea behind Test First Development is very simple: before you change the behavior of the production code you must have a failing test.

A failing test is immensely useful because it tells you when you are done. By shifting the traditional sequence of development around so that the tests are the first things that are created, developers get feedback about whether their code is correct within seconds of writing the code. This has a very dramatic effect on the feel of programming and goes a long way toward addressing concerns about the defect rate.

Test First Development is extremely incremental. Before writing a method, a programmer has to create a Unit Test that shows how the new method is intended to be used. The programmer then has to run the test and prove that it fails. The programmer then uses Simple Design to implement the method to make the unit test pass. Once the unit test passes, the programmer uses Refactoring to clean up the code to make it conform to all the rules of Simple Design. The unit tests make sure that the Refactoring does not alter the behavior of the code. The programmer then creates another failing unit test for the same method and then does some more Simple Design to make that test pass. This cycle continues until the method does everything it needs to be able to do.

Periodically the programmer will run the entire suite of unit tests to make sure that the newly added/changed methods have not broken any other functionality. By running the entire suite of unit tests, the programmer is performing a complete regression test to address fears about the defect rate and the system going sour. If something else has been broken, the tests will point to the problem so it can be corrected or will let the programmer know that his approach was incorrect and he needs to try a different implementation. Trying a different approach is not expensive because all that has been lost is the five or ten minutes it took to implement the changes.

A very interesting aspect of Test First Development is that it neatly addresses fears about staff turnover. The suite of unit tests is a safety net and repository of design decisions. Even if a new team member makes a coding mistake, it is highly likely that the suite of unit tests will detect the error.

The suite of unit tests also supports large-scale Refactoring. If the System Metaphor or Simple Design practices suggest that it is necessary to change the design of some classes fundamentally (for example, merge two similar classes or split a class into two or more distinct classes), the unit tests provide the safety net that makes this feasible. Without the safety net, the developers would be very reluctant to refine the design because, as all programmers know, *if you change it, you might break it*.

Acceptance Tests

Acceptance Tests (a.k.a. *Functional Tests*) are an integral part of incremental development as practiced by XP. All User Stories are supported by Acceptance Tests, which are defined by the On-site Customer. These tests address the fears that the business has been misunderstood.

The Acceptance Tests force the customer to dig deep into their domain knowledge and precisely state what the application should do in specific circumstances. In doing so, the customer defines the acceptance criteria for the requested features and clarifies the business rules for the developers.

Acceptance Tests support Test First Development by making sure that all requirements are rigorously defined as automated tests that either pass or fail. A user story is not complete until all of the associated acceptance tests pass, so they provide a sanity check on the developer-written Unit Tests. If the unit tests all pass but the acceptance tests are failing, the developers know that the unit tests have to be improved and the application fixed. The entire suite of acceptance tests addresses the risk that the system might go sour because when adding new functionality, the programmers have to make sure that they do not break any of the existing functionality. Running the complete unit and acceptance test suites is a strong guarantee that nothing has been broken.

These Acceptance Tests also address the risk of false feature-rich applications, because if a feature is not needed by these acceptance tests, the rules of Refactoring and Simple Design state that the programmers must delete the superfluous feature.

The Acceptance Tests also address the risk of schedule slips because they give an unequivocal answer about the state of the software. They provide direct feedback to the question, "Are we done yet?" Ron Jeffries has stated this unequivocally: "Every minute between when the programmer thinks the story is done, and when she has run the acceptance test and PROVEN that the story is done, is a minute the project is running out of control."[1]

The immediacy of this feedback is a distinguishing feature of Extreme Programming. For every iteration, the team can see the answer to the question, "Are we done yet?" by looking at the Acceptance Test scores. At the end of each iteration, the application is tested and ready for delivery. The team does not have to wait for the application to go through the quality assurance department to get back a prioritized bug list. At the end of each iteration, the feedback loop has already been closed. The answer to "Are we done yet?" is yes, so the team can confidently move on to tackle the next iteration and the user stories that the customer will choose for that iteration.

Open Questions

There is a lot of controversy surrounding the utility of automating acceptance tests. Some testing professionals question the value of automating these tests because on more traditional projects most errors are detected when the tests are being originally created. Few mistakes are found when the tests are repeated. Others have questioned the economics of the automated acceptance tests, suggesting that at some point the cost of maintaining the automated tests could become a drag on the productivity of the overall team.

Test First Development feels exceedingly strange for programmers when they first encounter it. In the old days, programmers used to pride themselves on the fact that they could write an entire program and have it compile error free the first time. Now they are expected to get lots of errors deliberately every day [Jeffries, 2001, p. 107–120]. Although this feels really natural for XP developers, getting developers even to attempt this style can be difficult.

Training developers to be good at defining tests could be a challenge. Yes, developers can easily write unit tests, but will these unit tests be comprehensive? Will the tests even be correct? Testing is a skill that

---

1. Jeffries, Ron. Agile Testing Mailing List. November 9, 2001.

can be learned, but in the first few months of adopting Extreme Programming, a team is likely to need lots of coaching in how to write good unit tests.

Although you would think that the Coding Standards practice could not be controversial, it is because it values the idea of clear code rather than well-commented code. The idea is that if you express the intention of the code by using well-chosen method and class names, then comments in the code are superfluous duplication and should be removed. It remains an open question regarding whether it is possible to Refactor all code to meet the Coding Standards such that internal comments are no longer necessary.

One challenge that every XP team should look at is whether they will have the courage to leave the internal comments in the code while they strive to refactor the code. Yes, clear code that directly expresses the intention is the goal, but will the team accept the imperfection of internal comments if the commented-on code expresses the intention better? This could be hard, because following the letter of the XP rules is often easier than following the values of Extreme Programming.

It is also debatable whether every XP team will remember that the rules about clear code do not mean that they should not write external comments and usage documentation. Yes, developers could look at the unit tests to determine how to use a method on a class, but clear documentation of the API is also useful. Well-written Javadoc-style comments for every public method are very useful, but can easily be overlooked in all of the debates about clear code.

What Can Other Approaches Learn From XP?

XP-style unit testing has already caught on in the Java community, and the JUnit testing framework [www.junit.org] is in wide use. XP-style unit testing frameworks are available for many programming languages, and the Ruby programming language [www.ruby-lang.org] distribution even ships with a unit testing framework. In addition, the complete suite of acceptance tests for the language, the "Rubicon," is available on-line for anyone wishing to test their installation [http://www.rubygarden.org/triple-r/index.html].

Many approaches espouse the idea of testable requirements, but few go as far as Extreme Programming in insisting that for every requirement the customer has to specify an associated set of test cases. Customer-specified tests would be a great addition to many approaches because although testers can specify the tests, without deep domain knowledge, they often miss things. The tests cover the types of mistakes programmers typically make but fail to probe deeply to ensure that the application works correctly to meet the real needs of the users.

In a similar vein, many approaches espouse the idea of regression tests, but rarely allow the time to create a complete regression test suite. The Test First Development approach changes all this because it requires a failing test before any code is modified. This means that if a tester reports a problem, the unit tests get updated to report the problem before the code is modified. Effectively, this means that a good regression test suite is created by the developers during the project. Although this may be seen as expensive, it saves time compared with the traditional approach of having a bunch of people manually "test" the application whenever changes are made. An automated regression test suite is also extremely useful when an application has to run on multiple platforms.

Summary

- ⬧ XP has a unique viewpoint on testing as well as programming.
- ⬧ Of all the practices of XP, Test First Development is the most counterintuitive of them all.
- ⬧ The idea behind Test First Development is very simple: Before you change the behavior of the production code you must have a failing test.
- ⬧ Test First Development is designed to give developers immediate feedback about the quality of the code.
- ⬧ The suite of unit tests is a safety net and repository of design decisions.
- ⬧ There is a lot of controversy surrounding the utility of automating acceptance tests.
- ⬧ Well-written Javadoc-style comments for every public method are very useful, but can easily be overlooked in all of the debates about clear code.
- ⬧ XP-style Unit Testing has already caught on in the Java community, and this "test infection" is spreading.

✧ Many approaches espouse the idea of testable requirements, but few go as far as Extreme Programming in insisting that for every requirement the customer has to specify an associated set of test cases.

Chapter 9

Working at This Intensity
Is Hard

Software development is supposed to be fun.

As you may have guessed, Extreme Programming is a high-intensity approach to software development. The planning practices are geared toward delivering maximal value in minimal calendar time. Delivering incrementally in short timeboxed iterations to exacting test standards is rewarding but difficult. Managed incorrectly, this could easily lead to burnout and staff turnover.

Because burnout and staff turnover are great ways to crash and burn any project, XP counters these pressures with practices that improve the social dynamics of the team. It ensures that software development is a truly collaborative process, both between programmers and between programmers and their customer. In addition, it recognizes that tired people tend to make mistakes, so it encourages the team not to work overtime. In this way the high-intensity work is balanced by a rewarding environment and adequate downtime.

Forty-Hour Work Week

At a time when many companies were trying to operate on Internet time, often putting in 60- or even 80-hour work weeks, XP was promoting the *40-Hour Work Week*, or the *No-Overtime rule*. The No-Overtime rule was interesting because of the way that it defined overtime as time you do not want to be at work. Given that standard, my guess is that there are some projects out there that wouldn't get many people showing up.

More recently, the practice has been renamed and is now called *Sustainable Pace*, but the concept is the same. Working too long and too hard increases the risk that the system will go sour as a result of a high defect rate, and simultaneously increases the risk of staff turnover. By focusing on the idea of a sustainable pace, XP emphasizes the need for long-term performance while still allowing for occasional overtime to deal with extraordinary events.

Pair Programming

Pair Programming supports and enables most of the other practices in Extreme Programming. It is also the practice that has the largest effect on how programmers work because it requires that all production code be written with a partner. Pair Programming is the mechanism that XP uses to ensure compliance with the rest of the programming practices, because with constant rotation among the pairings, the entire team can see who isn't really complying with the rules.

Pair Programming also turns out to be a great way of addressing the risks associated with bringing new programmers onto the team. Active pairing requires every pair to talk about the design, the requirements, the tests, and the code [Jeffries, 2001, p. 88–91]. By constantly rotating around into different pairings, knowledge is shared among the entire team so the hazards associated with staff turnover are lessened and new team members are quickly brought up to speed.

In addition, Pair Programming has a definite impact on the risk of a high-defect rate because pairing acts like a continuous code review. By continually trading the keyboard, the driving partner is always fresh and the reviewing partner can reflect on how the code that is being written fits in with the overall design.

On-Site Customer

Having an On-site Customer means that the risks of misunderstanding the business are minimized. It also enables the team to detect easily if the business has changed. The mere fact that the On-site Customer is colocated with the programmers makes an adversarial relationship unlikely, and hence reduces the risk of staff turnover.

Stress is also reduced for the programmers because they have someone who is always available who can clarify issues surrounding the requirements. This does, however, mean that the person or persons in the On-site Customer role have to have deep domain knowledge and sufficient authority to be able to make quick decisions about the overall direction of the project.

The On-site Customer role is extremely significant within an XP project. Yes, it is possible to bolster their domain knowledge by providing systems analysts to assist the customer, but the people in the role still have to be decisive enough to steer the overall project successfully.

Open Questions

Although the practice of having an On-site Customer is extremely beneficial for the programmers, it is questionable as to whether the customer is really working at a sustainable pace during an XP project. The problem is that the customer is expected to have really deep domain knowledge and to be able to answer programmers' questions decisively. In addition, the On-site Customer is expected to understand the organization's overall priorities so that she can effectively steer the XP project to deliver maximal value.

The XP literature to date has mainly focused on the technical side, and there is little written about how to perform the on-site customer role. Because it requires deep domain knowledge, it is not something the organization can delegate to junior end users. Experience with traditional projects suggests that it is rare to get enough access to senior people, so the availability of good customers may be a limiting factor in XP projects. Yes, it might be possible to use a more junior person in the On-site Customer role, but that would probably slow the project down as the junior customer gathers information and gets decisions ratified.

Given that the On-site Customer is also the person who holds the real vision for the system, it is also questionable as to whether it is possible to change the customer in the middle of a project. Needing to retain a single customer for the life of the project could restrict the applicability of XP, but changing customers could easily mean that the project is exposed to a radical business change in the middle of the project. Possibly this could be avoided by having a lengthy transition period, but there could still be chaos while they learn to "speak with a single voice."

Whether it is possible to do XP by replacing the On-site Customer with business analysts whose job is to collect the requirements and then represent the business to the programmers is open to question. Although some projects are attempting this, it exposes the project to risks related to misunderstanding the business and staff turnover resulting from tension between the now-remote customer and the programmers.

Pair Programming is a very controversial part of XP, and some programmers are going to be unwilling to even try the practice. True, most who try it for long enough report liking it, but there are some who are vehemently opposed to pair programming. Although there is some evidence that pair programming is more effective than working alone, more studies need to be done with experienced practitioners [Cockburn and Williams, 2001].

Interestingly, many of the objections to Pair Programming come from the mistaken idea that software development is a mechanical task. Hence, the assumption is that two people working on one task are inefficient and slow. It is an open question as to when this type of mechanical metaphor will cease to dominate thinking about software development [McBreen, 2002, p. 17].

It is also unlikely that the practice of using a Sustainable Pace will be acceptable in most organizations anytime soon. Historically, many (most?) software development projects have run on heroics and overtime, so an approach that is predicated on a sustainable pace will be hard to use in many organizations. Although there is some evidence that overtime is a cultural phenomenon [Cockburn, 2002, p. 107], it is an open question as to whether many organizations would adopt the practice of turning out the lights to encourage workers to go home.

Indeed, there is some evidence that some managers prefer to run "Death March" projects, if only to avoid the bureaucracy that comes with traditional project approaches [Yourdon, 1997, p. 34]. Some developers also reportedly enjoy the "hero" status that comes with successfully pulling off a death march project. Given this climate, the prospects for a sustainable pace are bleak. After all, as one reviewer put it, "management typically perceives that the reason the project is late is because of those blasted worthless programmers, so the blast of suffering is directed at the programmers, not at the sales people who made irresponsible promises" [personal communication, January 2002].

What Can Other Approaches Learn From XP?

A key idea that many approaches could benefit from is that face-to-face conversations reduce the risk of misunderstanding. Although documentation is useful as a static repository of requirements, developers get a much better sense of what is needed and wanted if they can actually talk to the users. Instead of having a full-time, on-site customer, other approaches that rely on business and systems analysts could still benefit from allowing the developers to talk directly to their end users.

Many approaches could benefit from the idea of an On-site Customer. All too many projects experience troubles because of insufficient contact, so being more assertive about requiring customer involvement is probably a good thing to experiment with. After all, there is sufficient anecdotal evidence to support the assertion that most projects could benefit from more customer involvement. Indeed, all of the Agile methods are very up front about stating the need for an actively involved customer.

A sustainable pace would probably benefit most projects. Although a "Death March" can sometimes be successful [Yourdon, 1997], the resulting burnout normally leads to staff turnover. On Death March projects, developers often end up making lots of mistakes and the team can end up having to talk about "good-enough software" to justify the fact that in trying to remove bugs, they will more or less certainly introduce more. The fallacy of good-enough software is that it is impossible to write bug free-software [McBreen, 2002, p. 56–57]. Although I would agree that it is practically impossible to write defect-free software at the unsustainable pace of a Death March project, well-rested developers working at a sustainable pace can come really close to writing defect-free software.

Choosing to work at a sustainable pace rather than in frenetic haste is a very valuable lesson from XP. The reason for this has been documented by Tom DeMarco in his book titled *Slack*. "The best predictor of how much work a knowledge worker can accomplish is not the hours that he or she spends, but the days. The twelve-hour days don't accomplish any more than the eight-hour days. Overtime is a wash." [DeMarco, 2001, p. 64] Yes, occasional overtime gives a short-term gain, but in the long term, quality is decreased and staff turnover rises [DeMarco, 2001, p. 65–68].

Many projects could benefit from the practice of having more than one pair of eyes see all production code. The practice of working together at a terminal did not originate with XP, and early anecdotal evidence was that working in "dynamic duos" produced code that "was nearly 100% bug-free" [Constantine, 1995, p. 118]. Although many approaches espouse the idea of design and code reviews, few projects use these frequently enough for them to provide any real, lasting benefit. Many organizations have launched initiatives to institutionalize inspections and reviews, but few find that these practices are sustainable in the long term. Indeed, a common lament is that "the inspections worked, quality improved, but for one reason or another the team just stopped doing them."

Some organizations have adopted the idea of "pair debugging." The idea is that a developer is allowed to struggle alone to find a bug for only a certain period and then must ask a colleague for help. This mitigates the risk of working late into the night to find the problem, only to give up in failure and then the next morning have a colleague instantly point to the source of the problem.

Summary

- ✧ Extreme Programming is a high-intensity approach to software development.
- ✧ The No-Overtime rule defines overtime as time you do not want to be at work.
- ✧ Pair Programming supports and enables most of the other practices in Extreme Programming.
- ✧ Pair Programming is a very controversial part of XP, and some programmers are going to be unwilling even to try the practice.
- ✧ The practice of having an On-site Customer is extremely beneficial for the programmers.
- ✧ All too many projects experience troubles because of insufficient contact, so being more assertive about requiring customer involvement is probably a good thing.
- ✧ A key idea that many approaches could benefit from is face-to-face conversations to reduce the risk of misunderstandings.
- ✧ Choosing to work at a sustainable pace rather than in frenetic haste is a very valuable lesson from XP.

Chapter 10

Is That All There Is to Extreme Programming?

Simple does not always imply easy.

Although it is simple to describe the practices, Extreme Programming is much more than the sum of all of the practices. The practices work synergistically in an environment that is set up to support the core values of Extreme Programming [Beck, 2000, p. 29–35]:

- ✧ Communication
- ✧ Simplicity
- ✧ Feedback
- ✧ Courage
- ✧ Respect

Of all of these values, respect is key. As Kent Beck states, "If members of a team don't care about each other and what they are doing, XP is doomed. So probably are most other approaches to writing software (or getting anything done), but XP is extremely sensitive to this." [Beck, 2000, p. 35]

Respect is the foundation of XP because, without respect, none of the other values are workable as a platform for organizing a team. Without respect, any gains the practices could give would be lost in the need to document, record, and justify everything that happens on the project.

Extreme Programming values courage because it is an approach to software development that trusts people more than it does a defined process. It takes courage to take the stand that communication supported by simplicity and concrete feedback can enable teams to deliver great software.

The approach works because all the practices work together to support the values. Small Releases and Acceptance Tests provide rapid, concrete feedback. On-site Customer, User Stories, Pair Programming, and the Planning Game all encourage lots of communication. Simple Design, Refactoring, Coding Standards, and the System Metaphor all support simplicity, whereas Continuous Integration and Test First Development give the team courage to move forward. The Sustainable Pace enables all of this because it allows time for respect.

Taken individually, each of the practices is probably a recipe for disaster on a project, but when supported by the other practices, the combination is very powerful. Keeping the appropriate balance between each of these practices is the reason that XP has been characterized as a high-discipline process. When everything is working well, successful XP projects seem to be able to deliver fantastic results.

Keeping an XP Project On Process

Although XP is a simple process, sticking to the process seems to be very difficult. As humans we are always trying to make life easier for ourselves, and in the process we drift away from what we know works. The temptation is that if we get away with slacking off once, then we can get away with slacking off all the time. Needless to say, this does not work very well.

To get around this problem, XP nominates someone to the role of a *Coach*. The job of the Coach is to ensure that all of the people on the project are keeping to the spirit of Extreme Programming. Although there are plenty of ways of measuring when an XP project is going off track, the job of the coach is to spot that the project is veering off course before the numbers are affected.

The Coach is an essential role because Extreme Programming is a highly tuned approach to software development. Even drifting slightly away from any of the practices can increase the defect rate or slow the team down. Without a coach, someone on a team will always come up with a reason for not doing a practice, and sooner or later this will cause problems [Auer, 2002, p. 264].

The coach is not there because you do not trust the team to do the XP practices. The coach is there to provide useful feedback to the entire team. As Ron Jeffries puts it, "Watch the people. You can spot trouble coming and avert it long before it will ever show up in your metrics." [Jeffries, 2001, p. 144] The coach provides the necessary mentoring and support to enable the entire team to become better developers as the project progresses. A useful side effect is that the productivity of the team remains consistently high throughout the project, because the coach is consistently looking for opportunities to improve the performance of the team.

One challenge for XP projects, though, is finding a developer who can be the full-time coach. Although the coach role is a high-touch, interpersonal role, the coach has to be a skilled, experienced developer who has seen enough projects to know what can go wrong. The coach has to be comfortable with talking to everyone on the team because it is his job to keep the conversation about the core values alive. Finding a suitable coach is a challenge because anybody who is qualified to be a good coach would also be a fantastic member of the programming team [Auer, 2002, p. 266–268].

The need for a coach may be a critical limitation of XP, if only because of the difficulty of locating qualified coaches. It may also put a restraint on how large an XP team can grow, because one coach can handle only so many people. After all, if there were 20 people in the team, at best the coach would have less than two hours with each person every week. With a team that large you would have to hope that most of the people already had in-depth XP experience so that most of the coach's time could be devoted to the few people who were learning XP.

You could argue, of course, that if the team was larger, then all you would need to do was have two or more coaches, but I doubt that would work. You would be very hard-pressed to find two coaches with compatible styles and intervention strategies who were available to work on the same project.

One last issue with having a coach is that they are very expensive to replace. The problem is that the entire team gets used to the personal style of their original coach, and switching to another coach is difficult.

In a sense, the problem is similar to that of the On-site Customer in that, ideally, the coach should sign on for the duration of the project.

Continuous Reflection

One essential task for an XP Coach is to ensure that the entire team continues to reflect on their process with a view to improving it. The idea that it is up to the team to improve its own process is a key contribution that XP has made to the conversation about software development.

This idea of continuous reflection is the reason why there is so much insistence in XP that a team start by following the rules. XP does not require the team to follow the rules blindly. Instead, it asks the team to start by following the rules and only then to try careful experimentation. The reason for this is that unless everyone is following the process, it is hard to determine if working off-process is the source of the problem or if the process itself needs adjusting. By bringing the entire team back to following the same set of rules, it is much easier to diagnose any problems.

Continuous reflection is also supported by the key meta-rule in XP: *They are just rules.* Teams are supposed to adjust and reformulate the rules actively to improve their own process. Each change in the rules should follow careful observation and reflection, and it should then be monitored to see whether the desired changes have come about. Hence, an XP team could decide that it is experiencing too much contention for the integration machine and that it needs to redefine what Continuous Integration means. If the team decides that code should only be integrated weekly, then the team would experiment with that and measure the results. If it made for a smoother running project with faster delivery and less stress, then that would become part of their new definition of XP. If, as is more likely, the results show slower delivery with more stress, strange interfacing bugs, and declining acceptance test scores, the team would revert back to the original definition of Continuous Integration.

The goal of continuous reflection is to keep the entire team actively engaged in trying to improve their process. When initially starting out with XP, a team is strongly encouraged by the XP community to follow the rules as written to establish a baseline level of performance. During this phase, a team is encouraged to reflect on how well their use of the practices matches the spirit of XP, to see how aligned they can become with the core values that underpin XP.

Experimentation with the rules should occur only after many iterations, because the rules have evolved from experiences on many different projects. Although there has been tweaking and tuning, the overall philosophy is the same: a small, colocated team that travels lightly to deliver maximal customer value in minimal time.

Distributed Development and Extreme Programming

Many people want to use XP practices in the context of a distributed team, but it is questionable whether it would still be XP if the team is not colocated. The argument is made that with decent communication links it is still possible to maintain "presence," but I remain unconvinced. Technology-assisted presence is sometimes effective for task-oriented communication, but even companies that sell state-of-the-art video conferencing technology rely heavily on face-to-face meetings in their own work [Cockburn, 2002, p. 93].

How the demand for distributed XP will be resolved is unknown, but distributed XP is being resisted. The idea that it is possible to do XP with a distributed team has led to the renaming of the On-site Customer practice to *Whole Team*. The idea behind Whole Team is that it emphasizes that all the contributors to an XP project sit together: all members of one team in one location. Using a distributed team is a less effective compromise than colocation. As such, a distributed team goes against the core values of XP, it uses a less effective means of communication, and all the necessary technology is nowhere near as simple as just sitting in the same room.

Open Questions

Requiring a coach for the effective use of XP on projects makes it harder for some organizations to really adopt Extreme Programming. Instead, many will attempt to run XP projects without a coach, and as a result will have projects that are using some of the practices of XP. This will lead to what Alistair Cockburn has termed *Pretty Adventuresome Programming* (see Chapter 15). The resulting project failures will doubtless cause confusion and concern regarding whether XP is faulty, or just that particular interpretation of XP was faulty. Although this is always a concern for any approach to software development, it is particularly a concern for XP because it encourages practitioners to tune the process to match their circumstances. My guess is that it requires developers with quite broad experience to create an appropriate variation on the XP theme.

The ability of a team to reflect on its own process is probably also extremely limited. The problem is that reflection requires idle time and, despite the intention to use a Sustainable Pace, I get a sense that most organizations prefer their developers to work at a frenetic pace. My guess is that few teams actively reflect on their process all that much because it requires adequate thinking time, and whenever developers stop to think, they no longer look "busy."

Haste and the need to look busy is such an endemic problem in organizations that Tom DeMarco wrote an entire book on the topic. *Slack* [DeMarco, 2001] addresses the need for a certain amount of slack time to allow people to think about becoming more effective, rather than just rushing around being efficiently busy.

What Can Other Approaches Learn From XP?

Following any process is not easy. As Jim Highsmith has often stated, "Having a process is not the same as having the skill to carry out that process." Many projects could learn from XP and have a full-time coach whose role is to assist the team in carrying out their chosen process.

One very interesting aspect of XP is its lack of specialization among the developers. Indeed, XP actively encourages a level of cross-training that is unheard of in most other approaches. This can be very useful because it lessens the risk that progress will be slowed as a result of having to wait for one key individual to perform a task.

XP is a good counterexample to the idea that role specialization is useful in software development. Although there are strong arguments in favor of specialization for mechanical tasks, the arguments for efficiency through specialization are inconclusive for intellectual tasks. By making the programmers responsible for doing their own design, XP avoids the inefficiencies and miscommunications that can arise when design ideas are passed from a designer to an implementer. Many of the arguments for this idea have been expressed by Jim Coplien in his "Architect Also Implements" pattern [Coplien, 1995, p. 205].

Explicitly naming the core values is a very valuable part of XP because it enables team members to make appropriate choices. Without this, it would be very easy for a team member to make a local change to their process that actually contradicts the overall intention of the espoused process.

To end this section on a controversial note, I find Extreme Programming very refreshing because of the way that Kent Beck [Beck, 2000, p. 35] highlights the importance of respect. It may be just me, but many of the issues I see in projects can easily be explained by the observation that the missing ingredient is respect. Sometimes it is as simple as a lack of respect within a team as the developers try to show that they are the "alpha geek." More commonly, the lack of respect shows up when the managers treat the development team as a bunch of interchangeable resources. Treating people as mere resources shows a lack of respect for the individuals, and once this mind-set is in place, it is very hard to get everyone to work together as a team.

Summary

- ✧ The practices work synergistically in an environment that is set up to support the core values of Extreme Programming.
- ✧ Respect is the foundation of XP.
- ✧ XP works because all the practices work together to support the values.
- ✧ Although XP is a simple process, sticking to the process seems to be very difficult.
- ✧ Following any process is not easy.
- ✧ XP actively encourages a level of cross-training that is unheard of in most other approaches.
- ✧ Extreme Programming is very refreshing because it highlights the importance of respect in building an effective team.

Part IV

Questioning XP Concepts

*When "It worked for us" meets "That will never work,"
bystanders get to see some great fireworks.*

Having looked at the practices of Extreme Programming and the factors that motivated those practices, the time has come to look at some of the underlying concepts. The criteria for inclusion here was simple: A concept has to be central to the controversies that have surrounded Extreme Programming ever since it was first announced.

If you have a "classical" software engineering background, many of these concepts are going to seem just plain wrong. Your challenge in reading this section is to look past what you already know and to try to see if there are any contexts and circumstances under which the idea could represent appropriate thinking.

If, on the other hand, you are a staunch supporter of Extreme Programming, all of these concepts will seem obvious. Your challenge in reading this section is to look past what you already know and to try to see if there are any contexts and circumstances under which the idea could represent inappropriate thinking.

If, on the third hand, you are one of the few people who are relatively neutral about Extreme Programming, I trust that this section spurs you to think about aspects of software development in a new light.

This section ranges over topics that include design, quality assurance, scalability of processes, change control and emergence, discipline, requirements, and maintenance. The discussion is grounded in the issues that software development projects face. The way that XP projects respond to these issues is compared with how other approaches respond to the same issues.

Chapter 11

The Source Code Is the Design?

Design is an activity, not a phase.

The claim that the source code is the design is one that has motivated many discussions about whether Extreme Programming projects really do design. Although the topic of design was covered in Chapter 7, it is useful here to try to understand the nature of the design activity in software development.

Jack Reeves [Reeves, 1992] explored this back in 1992 in an article titled "What Is Software Design?" Reeves compared software development with engineering disciplines to see how his understanding of engineering design mapped to software development. His conclusion was that, "we are not software engineers because we do not realize what a software design really is." He then went on to state the following:

> The final goal of any engineering activity is some type of documentation. When a design effort is complete, the design documentation is turned over to the manufacturing team. This is a completely different group with completely different skills from the design team. If the design documents truly represent a complete design, the manufacturing team can proceed to build the product. In fact, they can proceed to build lots of the product, all without any further intervention of the designers. After reviewing the software development life cycle as I understood it, I concluded that the only software documentation that actually seems to satisfy the criteria of an engineering design is the source code listings.

Admittedly, this is a controversial assumption, but using it Reeves managed to draw many interesting consequences from this assumption. The first blindingly obvious one is that software is amazingly cheap to build and to copy. Another is that small software designs are relatively easy to create (even if getting them right is difficult). The combination of these two means amazingly complex software is built using lots of small, easy-to-create software components. From this Reeves concluded that "Designing software is an exercise in managing complexity. . . . All of this makes software design a difficult and error-prone process." The design of a single class is relatively easy. It is the interactions between the myriad classes that are the challenge.

Although this is admittedly an obvious conclusion, it has many consequences for the way that we develop software. The next conclusion is more controversial and has much wider-reaching implications: *"It is cheaper and simpler to just build the design and test it than to do anything else."* This conclusion is the opposite from the mechanical world, because in the mechanical world, building and copying are expensive, slow processes. In software, building a design is a simple matter of running the compiler and linking the resulting code.

Software Development Is Mainly a Design Activity

The important observation that Reeves made was that "testing is a fundamental part of the design validation and refinement process." As such, most activities on a software development project are really design in a true engineering sense. Manufacturing is a very small part of any software development project, involving just the build, packaging, and distribution activities.

What makes this interesting from a questioning perspective is that if it is all design, when does it make sense to hand off the design work from one person to another?

- ✧ For large traditional software engineering teams, on long-running projects, handoffs occur from the business analysts to the systems analysts, from the systems analysts to the designers, from the designers to the programmers, and from the programmers to the testers. Along the way, many intermediate documents are passed around: requirements specifications, functional specifications, system design documents, program specifications, and test specifications.

Eventually, all these contribute to the production of the final, detailed design, which is the source code.

✧ In the context of an XP team, some handoffs do occur, even though they are supported by in-depth, ongoing conversations. The On-site Customer does hand off the requirements to the programmer and specifies the acceptance tests to a tester, and the tester hands off the acceptance tests to the programmer.

✧ From the perspective of a very small team on a short project, handoffs make little sense. The person who gathers the requirements can do the design work, and write and test their own code.

All three approaches are appropriate given the size of the team. Small teams require generalists who can take a project from start to finish in a very short time. Passing information from one person to another makes no real sense, because the time it takes to communicate all the necessary details just slows down the process. In the old days, the coding work would have been handed off, because programming used to be very slow. With a modern object-oriented programming language and a good development environment, the coding can be fast enough that a handoff is no longer necessary. In the time it would take to write a detailed program specification, the designer can have the program written and tested.

XP teams tackle larger projects, so it makes sense to specialize and have some handoffs. The choice that XP makes is to keep as many as possible of the design-related activities concentrated in one role—the programmer. It then makes the customer responsible for capturing the requirements and handing them off to the programmers and the testers, who are responsible for automating the acceptance tests. In this way, XP tries to function as much as possible like a very small team. It pays attention to testing because it recognizes that a design is not complete until it has been tested.

Large, traditional software engineering projects are organized around specialists and have many more handoffs. Specialization is necessary because of the size of the problems that are tackled. Understanding the problem domain is challenging, so a subteam has to specialize in understanding all the issues and figuring out how to communicate the essential complexity to the design team. Design requires a separate specialist subteam because of the complexity of the solution. For really large projects there can be multiple levels to the design, each one being validated before stepping down to the next level. Finally, the program specifications are written and validated before being handed off to the programmers. In parallel with this, the test team works with the requirements and design teams to create appropriate test specifications that will be used to validate the resulting source code.

Specialization is needed in these really large teams because it takes so long to come to grips with one aspect of the project that any skills in other areas of the project would easily get rusty. For a really complex business domain it can easily take an analyst a year to come to grips with and understand all of the nuances. As such, it makes sense for a person to specialize in doing analysis and domain modeling, because if she did attempt to do design or programming after spending a year doing nothing but analysis, she would be rusty. Far better that she focus on getting better at doing analysis. Similar arguments can be made for the system architects, designers, programmers, and testers. Specialization helps because there is enough of each activity to keep specialists busy full time in their own specialty.

Given all of this, it is easy to see why it is possible to say that "XP doesn't do design." It obviously cannot be doing design because all it has are programmers. There are no designers on an XP project and they do not produce any real design artifacts, so they cannot be doing design. Similarly, it is easy to see why XP teams sneer at the idea of doing "Big Design Up Front," because in their eyes a design is not complete until it has been coded and tested. It also explains why XP practitioners ask analysts and designers how much code they have written recently because, after all, "bubbles on a diagram cannot crash."

The specific concern that XP practitioners have with the Big-Design-Up-Front approach is that it can lead to large schedule slippage. The risk is that when the programmers get handed the design documentation, it is impossible to write the code. Although this risk is possible to circumvent by doing design reviews, many programmers have suffered at one time or another from incorrect design specifications.

The desire to deliver incrementally and to be able to support changing requirements are more reasons that XP discourages Big Design Up Front. By incrementally doing the design work, XP reduces the amount of work that has to be thrown away when the requirements change. Yes, features that have already been implemented will need to be reworked, but in XP there is minimal cost for changing requirements that have not yet been implemented. In contrast, with Big Design Up

Front, the design has to be reworked even if the feature has not yet been implemented.

Managing Complexity

The other conclusion that Reeves made was that "Designing software is an exercise in managing complexity" [Reeves, 1992]. Software development is hard because even small programs contain a lot of complexity; large programs are incredibly complex.

From a questioning perspective it is interesting to examine the different ways that the complexity is handled. How do the different hand-offs help or hinder the management of all the complexity?

⋄ From the perspective of a very small team, complexity is handled by choosing talented team members. The size of the problem that can be handled depends on the skill and experience the team members have with managing complexity. Teams also choose expressive programming languages and development environments that successfully manage to hide some of the complexity from the developers. Visual Basic is probably the most common environment for this type of team.

⋄ In the context of an XP team, complexity is handled by getting the customer to decompose the requirements into small chunks that can be handled within a short iteration. Then, by implementing using a very expressive object-oriented programming language, the programmers can handle more complexity. Through the System Metaphor, Simple Design, and Refactoring practices, XP projects seek to make the code as understandable as possible, and use Pair Programming to ensure that every programmer is familiar with most of the code. With copious tests to catch any mistakes, XP is capable of handling surprisingly complex problems.

⋄ For large traditional software engineering teams, complexity is handled through the division of labor and problem decomposition. The lead designer/architect identifies major subsystems and components, and designs the interfaces between these. Each module can then be handed over to another designer, who does the design of the components inside that module. Eventually, a low-level designer produces a detailed specification to hand off to a programmer to implement.

Each of these approaches has benefits and limitations. The small-team approach is very effective and productive for small problems, but fails miserably when the required complexity overwhelms the individuals. The XP approach has been shown to work for teams as large as 10 or 12 programmers working in expressive object-oriented languages, but has not been shown to work in low-level languages or for teams of more than 40 people. The traditional software engineering approach has proved to be effective for teams of 200 or more people, but seems to miss opportunities when applied to smaller teams.

One objection that XP practitioners have to the software engineering approach is that it makes it hard for programmers to contribute because all they ever see is a small piece of the picture. So rather than attempting to enable the programmers to understand the big picture and the overall design, the programmers are encouraged to focus on narrow pieces. The end result of this approach is more time spent in integration as the disparate pieces are brought together. Admittedly, more design and code reviews could help with addressing the integration issues, but there is always the risk of "shortcutting" the review process and only later discovering that there are different assumptions made on either side of an interface.

From the software engineering standpoint, it is hard to see how it is really possible for programmers to have the good understanding of the entire design that XP requires. After all, the programmers on traditional software engineering projects never seem to be able to grasp the overall design. XP, however, puts the programmers in daily contact with the On-site Customer so that they can understand the big picture. Then, through System Metaphor and Simple Design, the programmers can grasp and understand the overall design.

Why Now? What Has Changed?

The idea that the source code is the design was widespread in the Smalltalk community in the 1980s. Although it was not really articulated directly, few Smalltalk developers bothered with design documentation of the type seen in traditional software engineering projects. Instead, they talked about the objects and the messages they should send to each other, and in the end came to favor more informal approaches like CRC cards [Beck and Cunningham, 1989].

As object-oriented programming has become more popular, these ideas spread into the Java world as Smalltalk programmers started to use Java. Since then, the ideas have spread into the C++ world, and are also showing up in Python and Ruby projects.

In parallel with this, the software engineering world got interested in object-oriented development through needing design notations to support the constructs and concepts in Ada and C++. Eventually this led to the creation of the UML under the auspices of the Object Management Group [http://www.omg.org/technology/uml/].

With the increasing popularity of object-oriented development, these two cultures have ended up colliding. The software engineering world operates from the idea that the proper way to do design is to create a graphical model, validate the model, and then generate the code. The XP world operates from the idea that the proper way to do design is to express the design intentions directly in the code. One person went as far to suggest that "it is OK to use UML diagrams as long as you wash your hands afterward."

Currently there is very little middle ground between these two cultures. The problem is that the XP world values the expressiveness of the object-oriented programming language whereas the software engineering world would much prefer to be able to generate the code from UML specifications.

Scott Ambler is trying to create some middle ground by talking about Agile Modeling [http://www.agilemodeling.com/], but that appeals more to the software engineering practitioners than to the XP practitioners.

At the same time, many attempts are being made to create programming languages that allow the programmer to be even more expressive. In the past, when machines were very limited, it made sense to put the burden on the programmer to write code that suited the machine. Now it makes much more sense to have the machine do more of the work and to have languages that are much easier for people to use. Indeed, Yukihiro "Matz" Matsumoto, the creator of the Ruby programming language, has said

> ... *programming languages are ways to express human thought. They are fundamentally human-oriented.*
>
> *Despite this fact, programming languages have tended to be rather machine oriented. Many languages were designed for the convenience of the computer.*

However, as computers become more powerful and cheaper, this situation has gradually changed. For example, look at structured programming. Machines do not care whether programs are structured well. They just execute them bit by bit. Structured programming is not for machines, but for humans. This is true of object-oriented programming as well.

The time for language design that focuses on humans has been coming. [Fulton, 2002, p. xvi]

What Does This Mean for XP?

As tools and object-oriented programming languages get better, the complexity that can be handled by the XP approach will get larger. Similarly, as CASE tools and modeling notations get better, the software engineering approach will get better at handling smaller problems.

Our challenge will be to understand what happens in the overlap between the XP approach and the software engineering approach. We can expect to see much more controversy as these two approaches battle for mindshare. Over time, however, I expect that the two sides will start to recognize that the artifacts that the software development process produces, although useful intellectual property, are less valuable than the knowledge in the heads of the development team.

Many organizations already understand this, which is why they are always so keen to hire good developers away from their competitors [http://www.zdnet.com/eweek/news/1014/18ahejl.html]. Yes, the software and documentation are valuable, but the real intellectual property that allows the software to be revised and extended exists in the heads of the developers [Pavlicek, 2000, p. 102]. Documentation and clear source code are important, but their value is greatly enhanced by the ongoing conversations that exist within all effective software development teams. Although Extreme Programming shifts the focus toward the ongoing conversations, these conversations are still supported by written artifacts, just different ones than traditional processes would choose.

Summary

- ❖ XP considers testing a fundamental part of the design validation and refinement process.
- ❖ Smaller teams need generalists; larger teams can afford to use specialists in some roles.

- ✧ Designing software is an exercise in managing complexity.
- ✧ Programming languages can be made more human-oriented.
- ✧ However an eventual design is documented, in code or in models, the design is done by people.

Chapter 12

Test First Development?

Tests are great for showing that a feature is not yet implemented.

It has always been an article of faith that programmers cannot really test their own code because they know how it works. Strange as it may seem, Extreme Programming does not challenge this idea; instead, it tries to build on it. Test First Development requires that the Unit Test be written before the production code.

The idea is that before the method is written, the programmer does not know how it will work, so it is safe for the programmer to design the tests. After all, the programmer knows exactly what she wants the method to do, so it is simple for her to write a test that verifies that the method does the right thing.

But Do Programmers Know Enough About Testing?

The big question hanging over Test First Development is whether programmers know enough about testing for the unit tests to be effective.

One simplistic answer is that programmers can learn, but that avoids the question. The claim made by Extreme Programming is that the coverage provided by the Unit Tests enables the team to be very productive. The counterclaim made by the professional testing community is that the style of unit tests used by XP is not effective at capturing strange edge cases and interactions.

Although this debate still rages, it does appear that it is possible for a team to have reasonable confidence that practically all errors will be caught by a unit test suite. Although some errors will not be detected, the practice of enhancing the unit test suite whenever it is discovered that an error did slip through the test suite raises the overall confidence in the completeness of the unit test suite.

This confidence can also be justified based on the idea that the unit tests validate that all methods, given correct inputs, give the correct results. This simplifies the problem of assuring quality, because then all the team has to ensure is that the programmers use the methods correctly and that external inputs are validated before use.

Using the methods correctly is handled by requiring failing tests before production code is written, because it ensures that every method that is written has unit tests. If the methods that are called are used incorrectly, it is highly likely that the new method will not be able to pass its own unit test.

As for validating external inputs, that really comes down to having a good set of Acceptance Tests. Although these are primarily intended to be specified by the On-site Customer, the customer is assisted by a tester in making these tests reasonably complete. The person who has the role of tester in an XP team definitely needs to have a lot of knowledge about how to test software.

So is there a role for professional testers in XP? Yes and no. Yes, in that a professional tester could make a great contribution to the team, and no, in that working in XP-style iterations is contrary to normal testing practices. The problem is that testing has traditionally occurred at the end of the development process. Testers are used to getting a release, testing it, and passing issues and queries back to the development team. Few testers have experience working in short timeboxes during which the entire application plus revisions have to be tested every two or three weeks. Most testers are more used to manual testing, and it is just not feasible to retest an entire application manually that frequently.

The role of the professional tester is most closely aligned with that of the On-site Customer. Indeed, many XP teams have aligned their quality assurance and testing activities with the On-site Customer role. The testers work with the On-site Customer to assist in defining appropriate acceptance tests. The expertise of these testers then becomes available to the XP team in the form of a more complete suite of acceptance tests.

How Expensive Are Automated Acceptance Tests?

The accepted wisdom in the testing community is that automated acceptance tests are really worthwhile only if rerunning the test is likely to detect an error. The problem is neatly summarized by Brian Marick, who said, "What's hard about automated testing is that the product changes, which tends to break the tests. If you spend all your time fixing broken tests, was it really worthwhile to automate them?" [Marick, 1998]

The problem is compounded by the fact that creating automated tests costs more than creating manual tests, so the true cost of automated tests is the number of manual tests that are not performed (and hence bugs that go undetected).

An alternative viewpoint on automated acceptance testing is that it is qualitatively different from manual acceptance testing:

> *When you perform a test by hand, you bring to bear the entire range of human capabilities. You can improvise new tests or notice things that you did not or could not have anticipated. Test automation is a faint, tinny echo of that rich intellectual process. That's why it's nonsensical to talk about automated tests as if they were automated human testing. [Kaner, 2002, p. 99]*

The overall consensus in the testing community seems to be that automating unit tests is nearly always beneficial, but that the benefits of automating acceptance testing are very dependent on the situation. Some acceptance tests can and should be automated, especially for batch and system interfaces, but for applications with an extensive user interface, there is no substitute for skilled, experienced manual testers.

The counterargument that XP makes to this is that by starting with a very small system and building up the automated acceptance test suite every iteration, it is possible to create a good, automated acceptance test suite even for graphical user interface (GUI) applications. Effectively, what happens is that XP transforms what has traditionally been a time-constrained activity into one in which there are no real constraints. By ensuring that the automated tests are built incrementally, the tester's job is completely changed.

Effectively Defect-Free Versus Good Enough Software

By making sure that testing is not resource constrained, XP destroys one of the arguments for Good Enough Software [Yourdon, 1996]. XP teams have to keep their code defect free from the start, because all failing unit tests have to be fixed. Yes, the economic arguments from Good Enough Software about whether it is better to have more features or more robust software still apply, but in XP these are addressed by the On-site Customer. Extensive and comprehensive acceptance test suites will improve the overall robustness of the software, whereas less stringent acceptance tests may allow the team to develop functionality faster.

The key difference, however, is that with Test First Development, an XP team is not going to be faced with a massive list of outstanding bugs, so "bug triage" is not part of XP. All defects get demonstrated by a failing acceptance test. Then, before the programmer is allowed to change the code, a failing unit test has to be created. Once there is a failing unit test, it is normally very easy to fix the defect. It would be very hard for an XP project to claim an economic case for not fixing a defect.

The claim that is made by the XP community is that it is possible to create software that is effectively defect free. Yes, there may be some errors, but once detected they can be economically fixed. Over time, as the application gets more feature rich, the growing suite of tests should make the software even better, rather than the more usual case in which larger applications have more bugs. This has been seen at Symantec, where it was reported that "there were only five bugs found at beta, which was radical. By another measure, Orca today, after six months of development, had only 14 bugs across 13 [two-week] iterations." [Morales, 2002]

What About Code That Is Hard to Test?

Code that was written from the ground up with Test First Development is easy to test, but other code can be much harder to test. The challenge that XP teams face is that their code has good test coverage and they feel confident that it is solid. With other code, that confidence is not there.

Converting from a traditional project to an XP project is hard because the original code does not have XP-style unit tests. Although it may be feasible to create unit tests for the original code, this could take months, and in that time the team would not be delivering new features or functionality. In practice, what most teams try to do is to write unit tests only for code that they are modifying. Working with the rest of the untested code is still an issue, however, and an XP team could be tempted to push to restart the project from scratch to avoid the pain of dealing with the original code. Sometimes this can be a useful option, but the organization has to be sure that the existing code cannot be salvaged in order for this to be a realistic option.

When working with external libraries, the lack of unit tests can make it hard for an XP team to make progress. Because the unit tests have to run at 100 percent, problems with an external library can cause major headaches with getting the tests to pass. Over time, this will resolve itself as more and more libraries are shipped with XP-style unit tests, but until then there will always be some discussion as to whether it is better to use an external library or to create a robust version in-house.

GUI code probably tops the list as being very hard to test. All GUI libraries are large and complex, and most were not developed with the idea that programmers needed an easy way to test their applications. Although we now have capture/playback testing tools, these are of limited use because they interact only with the user interface. They cannot easily compare values in the running application with data displayed on the user interface. Currently, most teams resolve this by making the GUI code as thin as possible and by providing an alternate input mechanism for testing the user interface.

Can Acceptance Tests Be Used to Measure Progress?

One strange aspect of XP is that it uses acceptance test scores as a measure of project progress. Although user stories are used to plan the work for each iteration, completion of a user story is measured by the associated acceptance tests.

The basic idea is that if testable requirements are a good idea, then making the tests the requirements is an even better idea. The obvious downside to this is that the On-site Customer has to have really deep domain knowledge so that they can help the testers create good acceptance tests. It also puts a lot of pressure on the testers to keep up with the iteration plan. Every iteration, the testers have to create acceptance tests for every user story in that iteration and have those tests available before the programmers need them.

The problem for the testers is that these acceptance tests are the specification of what has to be delivered. Once all the acceptance tests pass, the programmers have delivered on the story. So the challenge for the testers is to create a very wide range of tests that cover all possible uses of the application. Just having lots of tests is insufficient; what is needed are tests that really probe the application.

One intriguing aspect of this is that if XP is being used to replace an existing system, generating a good set of acceptance tests is not too hard. Indeed, under these circumstances a team could probably release the new application to live use as soon as the complete suite of acceptance tests passes. Hence, it makes sense to use the acceptance tests as a measure of progress. In the case of a new system, for which there is no existing source of "correct" results, generating an appropriate set of acceptance tests will be much harder. On this type of project, the On-site Customer will probably need much more support from experienced testers if the acceptance test suite is going to be effective.

Does XP Do Proper Testing?

Some parts of the testing community see their job as that of trying to "break the product" for the benefit of their clients—that testing is about finding problems. They do not see testing as a preventive mechanism, but as a final inspection gate through which the software must pass. Unfortunately, this attitude is completely at odds with the way that XP sees testing as a error-prevention mechanism.

One consequence of this difference in opinion is the debate that continues to rage over how effective the testing is in XP. One interesting aspect of this controversy, however, is that the debate surrounding Test First Development has exposed many developers to new ideas about testing [http://www.testing.com/agile/] and has caused the testing community to reflect on their role in projects [http://www.testinglessons.com/].

In practice, although XP-style testing may not be as good as it possibly could be as far as the testing community is concerned, many organizations that adopt XP are discovering that the quality of the resulting applications is better. In part, this can probably be attributed to the fact that XP teams devote more effort to testing activities than many traditional teams.

Why Now? What Has Changed?

Moores Law is at the root of these changes. Traditional software engineering was founded in an era when computers were fantastically expensive and the turnaround on the batch compilation of programs was very slow. Veterans of that era often joke that you could get fired for needing too many compilation runs to get a program working. Even into the middle 1980s, large programs could take several hours to compile. Small wonder programmers got really good at desk checking programs for syntax errors before submitting the code to the compiler.

During the last few years things have changed. Computing power is so cheap that most programs can be recompiled in a few seconds, and it is rare for even large applications to take more than ten minutes to build. Hence, time spent desk checking for syntax errors is now wasted time, because the compiler will find all problems in a few seconds and position the cursor for the programmer to fix the offending line.

It is now more effective to let the computer do the work. With expressive, dynamic object-oriented languages like Smalltalk, Python, and Ruby, and faster machines giving shorter compile cycles in object-oriented languages like Java and C++, it is realistic to type a few lines of code and then run the tests without interrupting flow.

Also, as discussed in Chapter 2, the Smalltalk community had proved the effectiveness of unit testing as a means of detecting errors. As object-oriented development became popular, ideas from the Smalltalk community spread as Smalltalk programmers worked in other languages and talked to fellow developers. Hence, what the Smalltalk community had learned about test first development spread to the rest of the object-oriented community. Indeed, the popular JUnit unit testing framework [`http://www.junit.org`] was created because, at the time, Java lacked a unit testing framework similar to Smalltalk's SUnit.

What object-oriented developers are learning is that writing the tests first makes it easier to understand what the code is supposed to do. This happens because the developer has to think how the various objects will be used rather than thinking about how to make the class easier to implement. The side effect that it also makes the classes easier to test is a pure bonus from a programming point of view. The extension of the unit tests to end-to-end acceptance tests is a natural idea that supports the flexibility so valued by programmers.

What Does This Mean for XP?

As Kent Beck has stated many times, XP testing is about demonstrable confidence [Beck, 2000, p. 115]. The general idea is that "you should test things that might break" [Beck, 2000, p. 117]. Although this may seem to produce tests that are very weak compared with what is possible given experienced testers creating detailed tests, in practice it means that XP projects have better testing than most other projects.

The challenge for XP projects is to find a way to get experienced testers to work with the on-site customer as part of the XP team. This will require changing perceptions about XP in the testing community, but the end result should be even higher quality applications. After all, an experienced tester working with the customer should be able to produce better tests than a programmer who is temporarily in the role of tester. Even better, when the acceptance tests detect a problem, an experienced tester will be able to help the programmers get better at writing their unit tests. The challenge is to make testers an integral part of the software development process, rather than after-the-fact commentators and critics, as in the traditional approach.

Summary

- ✧ Test First Development requires that the Unit Test be written *before* the production code.
- ✧ Automated acceptance testing is qualitatively different from manual acceptance testing.
- ✧ The overall consensus in the testing community seems to be that automating unit tests is nearly always beneficial, but that the benefits of automating acceptance testing are very dependent on the situation.
- ✧ By making sure that testing is not resource constrained, XP destroys one of the arguments for Good Enough Software.
- ✧ The XP community claims is that it is possible to create software that is effectively defect free.
- ✧ Converting from a traditional project to an XP project is hard because the original code does not have XP-style unit tests.
- ✧ XP uses acceptance test scores as a measure of project progress.
- ✧ Many object-oriented developers are learning that writing the tests first makes it easier to understand what the code is supposed to do.

Chapter 13

Large-Scale XP?

A team of 20 developers is a large team.

Although XP can probably scale to large-size problems [http://www.thoughtworks.com/library/XP On A Large Project-A Developer's View.pdf], it was never intended to be used with large teams. Kent Beck [Beck, 2000, p. 157] suggested that even a team of 20 programmers would be a stretch. A realistic team size limit for XP is probably 12 programmers. So the real question is, how big a problem can a team of that size handle?

Are Large Teams a Goal?

Although the traditional approach to software development has involved throwing as many bodies at a problem as possible, maybe there is another way. Small teams working in an environment that is conducive to learning can achieve extraordinary productivity.

So does it really matter if XP is limited to small teams if it can still deliver the necessary functionality? For some organizations it does matter, because there is less reward for managing a small team than for managing a larger team. Although this may seem strange, it is nonetheless true. For some organizations, the status of a manager depends on the size of the team managed, not on what the team accomplishes. In cases like this, XP is probably an inappropriate choice for the organization. Other organizations would probably choose to use a smaller team.

A key question for which there is no supporting data is, how much more productive is XP? Various claims have been made, but nothing definitive can be said. It would, however, be very interesting to assemble a team of ten experienced XP programmers to see how productive they could be. But then again, if you ever manage to assemble a team of ten experienced developers, you would probably discover that they were much more productive than any of your other teams anyway.

Long-Running Projects

As experience builds with long-running XP projects, we may discover that it is possible to build really large, complex systems using small XP teams. To date, this is only speculation, but there is some evidence that suggests that XP projects do not slow down as time progresses. Given that this is true, there is reason to believe that the XP practices manage to stave off the "code rot" that affects many other projects. This is only to be expected given the emphasis that XP places on ensuring that the code is maintainable.

So although XP does not scale in terms of team size, it looks like it will scale successfully in terms of team and project duration. XP teams seem to be able to handle some staff turnover, at least on the programmer side. There are still some open questions as to how easy it is for an XP project to survive turnover in the customer and coach roles.

Coordinating Multiple Teams

Not content with the idea that XP is limited to small teams, some organizations have tried to find ways to have multiple XP teams working in parallel on related projects as a way to scale XP [Crocker, 2001]. The basic idea is that if a problem can be partitioned well enough, then it can be worked on independently. So, in a sense, these organizations are trying to apply XP within a traditional software engineering approach.

Mike Beedle, one of the authors of Scrum, has also been experimenting with XBreed, a combination of XP and Scrum. Scrum handles the overall coordination of the projects and XP handles the development process inside each of the sprints.

Although these extensions to Extreme Programming are interesting in their own right, they are just natural attempts to fit what is essentially a project process into the larger organizational context. Organizations have always faced the problem of coordinating many projects, and with the rise of Extreme Programming, the challenge will be to coordinate between different styles of projects as well.

Personally, I have doubts as to whether using multiple XP teams to create parts of a larger system is really the way to tackle projects that are beyond the scope of XP. The early partitioning of the problem so that separate teams can work on their own chunk seems contrary to the spirit of XP, because there does not appear to be an easy way to get feedback as to whether the initial partitioning is effective.

Is It OK for a Process to Have Limits?

This is the big unasked question. Does it really matter if a process cannot scale to large teams? One answer would be that the process needs to scale in case the project is very successful and the team has to grow to support a massive user community. Admittedly, this is probably a long shot, but it could be a legitimate concern for some organizations.

My answer to the scaling issue is that I'm much more comfortable with approaches that try to solve one set of problems than approaches that claim to be able to handle all sizes of problems. The single-size approaches are easier for teams to deal with because they require much less adjustment. One-size-fits-everything approaches require a lot more adjusting, and few teams have the necessary experience in tailoring to make successful adjustments.

Although the scaling arguments tend to look at larger size teams, the same also fits for smaller sizes. For many projects I would venture to suggest that XP is, in fact, too large. For teams of less than four programmers, XP is probably overkill because the coach and customer would be underutilized. It would be hard to justify locating the customer with the programming team when, in fact, the programming team cannot keep the customer reasonably busy. The coach would be underutilized as well, and although this would allow the coach to participate more in development, it would be very easy for the team to drift away from the practices.

Overall, I would suggest that XP is best suited to projects with a narrow range of team sizes, probably 4 to 12 programmers. Outside that range, other processes are probably more appropriate. The good news, however, is that a great many projects fall into the range of applicability.

Indeed, there is some evidence that XP-size projects are predominant in the industry. There are some large, 1,000-person, billion-dollar projects out there, but they are quite rare.

Why Now? What Has Changed?

How come it is suddenly possible to deliver many projects with comparatively small teams? It seems to be a combination of factors. Organizations are very wary of big projects, so most projects are on the small side. With software development shifting to object-oriented languages, the functionality available in the class libraries has made it easier for small teams to deliver bigger systems. This is not so much a case of software reuse within an organization, but more the availability of components and class libraries that a project can effectively utilize.

In addition, object-oriented languages tend to be more expressive, so less code is required for equivalent functionality. Small teams of developers who really know the class libraries well can be extraordinarily productive by leveraging the power of the existing libraries.

What Does This Mean for XP?

Because it is not really feasible to use larger teams in XP, teams have to find a way to deliver more value in the available time. The best way to do this is to follow the advice given by Jim Highsmith: "Start Earlier." [Highsmith, 2000, p. 301] By avoiding wasting months and months during the early inception phases of a project, XP projects effectively start earlier and hence have more time to deliver essential functionality. With partial functionality in live use, it often turns out that the rest of the functionality can be delivered slightly later than was originally requested [Gilb, 1988, p. 101].

Another way to work with small teams is to make sure that every team member is talented and has lots of experience. Although this strategy is not always feasible, keeping a team intact is a great aid to productivity [McBreen, 2002, p. 145]. Communication within the team is much more effective because the programmers know each other really well.

The last way to avoid the need for larger teams is to make sure that the XP team has the best possible tools and development environment. By enabling them to leverage the power of object-oriented languages, access to good class libraries helps by reducing the amount of code that has to be written. Rather than have the XP team waste time building infrastructure code, the organization should seek to leverage whatever is already available. Although this may seem to be a contradiction that flies in the face of Simple Design, it is not if the simplest way to deliver the functionality is to use what someone else has already created.

One open question that remains, however, is what would a two-person team version of XP look like and would it be useful?

Summary

- XP was never intended to be used with large teams.
- Does it really matter if a process cannot scale to large teams?
- One-size-fits-everything approaches require a lot more adjusting, and few teams have the necessary experience in tailoring to make successful adjustments.
- Because it is not really feasible to use larger teams in XP, teams have to find a way to deliver more value in the available time.

Chapter 14

Is the Cost of Change Really Low?

The economics of software development are weird.

The cost of change controversy is such an important part of the debate over Extreme Programming that it needs to be looked at in detail. As we saw in Chapter 1, the assumption that the cost of change is exponential is just that, an assumption. There is no real data one way or another about the cost of change in modern software.

The original evidence for an exponential cost of change came from Boehm's book *Software Engineering Economics* [Boehm, 1981, p. 40–41]. What most people miss when they read this reference is that there are actually two lines on the famous graph. One supports the well-known assertion that various factors combine to "make the error typically 100 times more expensive to correct in the maintenance phase on large projects than in the requirements phase." There is also a dotted line of the graph that shows data from two smaller, less formal projects. Boehm states, "Although the effect for smaller projects is less pronounced, the 4:1 escalation in cost-to-fix between the requirements phase and the integration and test phase supports [the] premise."

Interestingly, even Boehm suggests that sometimes "it may be more cost-effective to proceed with development of a first-cut prototype product rather than spend more effort pinning down requirements in full detail. . . . An even stronger case for the prototype approach can be made for small, informal projects with their 4-6:1 cost-to-fix increase, and for problem domains in which rapid prototyping capabilities are available."

I would contend that modern object-oriented development environments are way more powerful and productive than the prototyping environments that were available back in 1981. Couple this with the Test First Development practices and it would be easy to imagine that a team could do better than a 4:1 cost-to-fix increase.

What Is the Cost of a Requirements Change?

Estimating the cost of a requirements change is not easy because it depends on the approach used. In a traditional approach, we have to factor in the cost of the initial analysis work and the probability that the analysts would have been able to predict the change. This probability is low because users tend to be certain about what they need until they see the real thing, at which point new ideas come up. Indeed, on some projects I have worked on, it was the things that the users were most certain about that ended up changing.

We also have to factor in the costs of the design documentation, programming, and testing. Although a requirements change could be noticed at any point during the development process, typically the mismatch between the application and the real business process is only noticed near the end, when the users start acceptance testing or, even worse, when the application goes live. Then, depending on the rigor of the approach, either the code is just fixed up or the requirements documentation is changed, and the resultant changes are then rippled through the entire system.

Although quick-and-dirty code changes are very common, they has the awkward side effect of invalidating all the other documentation, so they are usually frowned upon. On the other hand, going back and updating the requirements documentation and pushing that back through the development process is expensive, because the implications of the change must be investigated. If the team has maintained requirements traceability, then finding the impact is easier, but we then have to factor the cost of originally tracking all requirements into the cost of change.

The cost of a requirements change is different for Extreme Programming because the activities and timescales are different. It spends much less time up front trying to validate the requirements and instead gets the functionality into the hands of the users as quickly as possible. This provides very rapid feedback to the On-site Customer so that the project can be steered toward creating a useful application. By involving the On-site Customer in the development process, XP addresses the problem of partial knowledge in the requirements. By developing in small increments, XP allows the On-site Customer to learn about the evolving application and how to communicate effectively with the developers.

The cost of requirements change is also lowered by incremental development because, unlike the traditional approach, requirements changes are essentially free for all functionality that has not yet been implemented. All that needs to happen is that the appropriate user story gets rewritten, whereas in a traditional project, the requirements documentation needs to be reworked, and the impact traced into any design and code that has already been worked on.

Requirements changes for functionality that has already been delivered are also cheaper. Working with the partial application, the On-site Customer has to work out what should be different, rewriting user stories, adding new user stories, and removing obsolete stories. These stories then get sequenced into the overall release plan so the cost of the requirements change is the amount of work that has to be slipped to fit in the necessary changes.

The most usual case for a requirements change occurs during an iteration. As stories are implemented and tested, users see there is a mismatch between the application and the real business process. Resolving this is cheap, because the programmers are currently working on the functionality, so it is easy to adjust the current story to match the real business process. At worst, some stories may need to be deferred to the next iteration. If the new features suggest additional, useful functionality, then new user stories are added into the release plan and, as we have already seen, these are essentially free.

Hence for XP, the cost of requirements change is the cost of the original user story and the changes necessary to support the "real" user story. Because all user stories cost between one and three programmer weeks (this is a game rule for XP), the worst case is a change request cost of between one and three programmer weeks for every affected user story. So yes, a change that affects many user stories could be expensive, but the cost should be proportional to the number of stories affected. As such, the cost of a change may be easier to explain to the customer than when using the traditional approach.

The traditional approach and XP are both successful strategies in their own field. XP seems to match fast-moving businesses and emergent requirements better (see Chapter 16) because it has a lower cost of change when the change could not have been predicted. The traditional approach is probably better in more stable environments, in which the requirements are well-known and change is easier to predict.

What Is the Cost of Fixing a Bug?

For most projects, the cost of finding a bug is much larger than the cost of fixing the bug. Indeed, in many cases, once a bug has been isolated, the fix is trivial. The expensive part is detecting and then isolating the bug. Of course, it is possible to write software in a way that makes it practically uneconomical to fix bugs, because that is the overall justification behind the idea of Good Enough Software; but normally, bugs are easy to fix.

One hidden cost of bugs is the expense that users incur in reporting and dealing with the bug until it is eventually fixed. With some unhealthy organizations, users face an uphill struggle in getting the developers even to acknowledge that the software is not working correctly—the *"that is not a bug; it is a feature"* conversation. Users then face additional costs while they have to work around the bug until a permanent fix is installed, and in many cases these costs can drastically outweigh the costs that development teams face in fixing the bug.

To understand the development team's cost of fixing a bug, we must first distinguish between two sources of defects. Errors of understanding can occur when developers or the On-site Customer misinterpret the real needs of the users. Design errors, on the other hand, occur when the developers understand what they are supposed to create but make a mistake and implement the feature incorrectly.

What Is the Cost of Fixing a Design Error?

Design errors are mistakes that the developers make; things like coding errors, incorrect unit tests, inappropriate design choices, clumsy user interfaces, and incorrect documentation.

The Unit Tests in XP make isolating coding errors much easier than in traditional projects. I can attest to this from personal experience, because after shifting to writing XP-style unit tests I found that I no longer needed to use a debugger to step through code line by line trying to locate bugs. The change has been considerable. Ten years ago I knew practically every command in the debugger and used it several times a day. Today I use a debugger maybe three or four times a year.

Interestingly, even incorrect unit tests are not a major issue because whenever you get a disagreement between the code and the unit test, you quickly learn that what matters is the disagreement between the results. Yes, it is normally the code that is incorrect, but every so often you discover an incorrect test result. The worst that can happen is if the unit test is incorrect and the code is written to match that incorrect test. This delays the discovery of the mistake until the incorrect method is invoked from another method, at which point the error is normally detected. The final check is when the acceptance tests are run, because these tests will fail if a method is returning incorrect values.

Inappropriate design choices are harder to detect but the emphasis on Simple Design and Refactoring ensures an XP team is always trying to refine and improve a design. The Acceptance Tests also help to resolve design errors because they can detect problems with poor performance very early on in the project. The cost of this type of error is lower in XP because if performance is a critical issue there will be acceptance tests that measure the overall performance available right in the first iteration. This is in marked contrast to some traditional projects in which actual measurement of the performance typically happens only toward the end of the project, when it is often too late to correct the mistake without major rework.

I know of one project—which has to remain nameless—where an intranet Web development team used a technology that was not available on the corporate intranet servers. Large parts of the application had to be rewritten before it could be deployed because it was not feasible to change the corporate servers to fix the mistake made by the team. By using Small Releases, XP reduces the cost of fixing design errors that really only show up when real users get their hands on the application. If the initial release has a poor user interface or inaccurate user documentation, it is very easy for the On-site Customer to use this information to redirect the developers to fixing these issues early, when the cost is lower.

What Is the Cost of Fixing an Error of Understanding?

Finding these types of mistakes is expensive in all approaches to software development. XP does this through Test First Development and the Acceptance Tests; other approaches use various combinations of reviews, inspections, and testing. When applied diligently, the approaches are probably equal in effectiveness, so the real differentiator between approaches is how well they perform under typical project circumstances.

The difference here is that XP sees testing as a preventive mechanism that is part of the overall development process, whereas many other approaches have a final inspection approach. *When* an error is found really affects the cost to fix it. With testing seen as final inspection, the cost to fix it can be high because of the time lapse before the error is detected. With testing as a preventive mechanism, detection of the bug occurs within hours (or at worst, days) of the code being written, and the cost to fix it can be low because the programmer is still working on the code.

A larger issue, though, is that when testing is seen as a final inspection, there is always pressure to cut back on the testing effort because it is seen as nonproductive. A common end result is that more defects slip through the testing net and end up affecting end users. This is less likely to happen with testing seen as a preventive mechanism because it is an ongoing activity that is an integral part of the development process.

Errors that slip through to affect end users are expensive to fix. Unless the team is doing very frequent XP-style incremental releases, it is likely that a lot of time has elapsed between when the code was written and when the error was detected. The longer the time that has elapsed, the harder it will be for programmers to find the mistake because they will be less familiar with the code.

XP reduces the cost of fixing bugs by requiring a failing test that demonstrates the defect. Although this could be expensive to create, it means that the programmers can easily rerun the tests to determine whether they have actually fixed the problem. This is in marked contrast to normal projects, in which a programmer can make a change and not know whether it has fixed the problem or whether it has introduced new problems. Rather than having an automated test suite that can verify the application, the programmer has, to instead, pass the application off to the test team for testing. The delays involved in this handoff and manual testing add to the cost of fixing bugs.

Overall, the cost of fixing errors of understanding is closely related to the time that elapses between making the mistake and detecting the mistake. If an error is made in capturing the requirements and lots of design documentation, program specifications, test plans, user documentation, and source code are written based on this mistake, then there will be a lot of rework to do. This is especially true if the mistake is discovered in acceptance testing a year after the mistake was originally made. XP, on the other hand, minimizes the time that can elapse between the mistake and detection by insisting on Small Releases. Every two weeks a new release is made available for the users to test. At worst, all that has to happen is that two weeks of work has to be fixed, which is obviously much cheaper than fixing an entire year's worth of work.

What Is the Cost of a Release?

One area in which the cost of change is still high is when a change involves making a new release of the software. To determine these costs, we have to include the costs of a release for the development team and for the user community.

With a good automated test suite, the costs of a release to the development team are dominated by the cost of distribution. On the other hand, if a lot of manual acceptance tests have to be run, then these costs might swamp the distribution costs.

For the user community costs we have to realize that the costs are not just measured in monetary terms. Even with the availability of the Internet as a mechanism for distributing fixes, we have to realize that every user will lose some time installing the upgrade. Although this can probably be managed for some internal applications, this would be harder to achieve for the large, distributed user community that is typical for most applications.

We could make the claim that a Web application has zero distribution cost for the user community because once the application server is updated, all users get the new application. While this may be true, the total costs may be more because Web applications typically have worse usability than normal applications, if only because of the time lost waiting for the screen to repaint inside the browser. So, in the search for cheaper distribution costs, larger hidden costs are passed on to the user community.

In the face of this, we should make the assumption that every release is expensive for the user community. As such, we should seek to avoid the need for bug-fix releases as much as possible. Incrementally releasing features is different because the added functionality is valuable and hence repays the investment in installing the release.

In practice, many XP teams cut a release every two weeks for a small group of users who do the final acceptance test of each Small Release [http://www.infoxpress.com/reviewtracker/reprints.asp?page_id= 970]. Only when that group is satisfied does the XP team distribute the application to the entire user community. This minimizes the cost of disruption while still providing adequate feedback from real users.

Why Now? What Has Changed?

A lot has changed since Boehm did the research and wrote his book. Good object-oriented languages make it easier to change and modify code because design decisions can be encapsulated inside classes. Good test harnesses reduce the cost of change because they massively reduce the time taken in debug.

The Internet has made it easy for the development team to distribute fixes, so the perception is that releases are cheaper. Unfortunately, this is not really the case. Yes, it is easy to distribute fixes, but each bug-fix release impacts the reputation of the development team. Although currently most software development teams currently have a poor reputation for quality and reliability, as soon as some teams start to deliver reliable software, the environment will change. Teams are going to have to pay a lot more attention to ensuring that as few defects as possible slip through to the end user while at the same time being very responsive to change requests.

Organizations are also starting to pay attention to the opportunity costs involved in delayed and buggy software. Projects are no longer measured purely by how well they meet their budget goals. The better organizations are now starting to measure the overall impact the project has on the rest of the organization. Projects that are able to respond quickly to requested changes are becoming preferable because they minimize the costs to the user community. In some cases, the opportunity costs of slow changes are so significant that it is cost-effective to run an inefficient, overstaffed software development team. Paying for a few extra developers is cheap when balanced against the value of being able to respond rapidly to change.

What Does This Mean for XP?

It may indeed be that the exponential cost of change identified by Boehm does not actually occur for XP projects. Interestingly, it seems that a flatter cost of change is made possible through the use of incremental requirements capture coupled with incremental development. If this is true, then the flexibility and responsiveness claims made for Extreme Programming can be realized by any approach that practices incremental requirements capture and uses a short delivery cycle—for example, Scrum, DSDM, and Feature-Driven Development.

The key, though, is to ensure that each release is rock solid so that incremental bug-fix releases are not required. The reason for this is that each release can have significant costs in terms of user disruption, for which most software development projects do not usually have to account.

Summary

- ◆ The cost-of-change debate is not going to be settled anytime soon.
- ◆ Estimating the cost of a requirements change is not easy because it depends on the approach used.
- ◆ XP seems to match fast-moving businesses and emergent requirements better because it has a lower cost of change when the change could not have been predicted.
- ◆ With XP, the cost of a change may be easier to explain to the customer because it should be proportional to the number of affected stories.
- ◆ Errors that slip through to affect end users are expensive to fix.
- ◆ XP reduces the developer cost of fixing bugs by requiring a failing test that demonstrates the defect, but creating this test may be expensive.
- ◆ When looking at the cost of change we have to look at both the development team and the user community.
- ◆ Projects that are able to respond quickly to requested changes are becoming preferable because they minimize the costs to the user community.

Chapter 15

Setting the Dials on Ten

My methodologist is bigger than your methodologist.

One characterization of Extreme Programming is that it attempts to minimize what can be described as non-value adding activities while it maximizes value-added activities. "Setting the dials on ten" is the way that Kent Beck [Beck, 2000] describes taking practices that are known to be effective and taking each to its logical conclusion.

Although it is easy to parody, as many have done, the idea that if something is good, doing more will be even better, and this could make us ignore a useful innovation—that a set of practices can be synergistic. The synergy between the practices is what makes Extreme Programming different. It also makes XP seem very dogmatic because, as Beck explains, "there is much more to be gained when you put all the pieces in place." [Beck, 2000, p. 150]

Interestingly, though, there is a lot of controversy over deciding which activities can be classed as non-value adding. In a sense, it comes down to the fears that the approach is meant to mitigate. Anything that does not really address your fears can easily be classed as non-value adding for your project, but another team with a different set of fears would call the same activities essential for the success of their project.

What About the Overdose Effect?

Although it may be possible for an overdose of any one practice to have a detrimental effect on a project, the question we first have to ask is whether it is possible for an overdose to occur. Yes, a team could overdose by doing only a subset of the practices, but provided they do all the practices, it would be very hard to overdose.

The reason why it is hard to overdose on any one of the practices is because the discipline of Small Releases combined with Pair Programming keeps everyone focused on delivering useful functionality. Within this context, an overdose of any practice that slowed down delivery would be easily detected and corrected. Through pairing, programmers learn what Simple Design really means, how to Refactor, and how to write appropriate Unit Tests.

The role of the XP Coach is to ensure that the team stays productive. An experienced coach would see the team putting too much attention on one practice and ignoring others, at which point the coach would remind the team about the overall process. During the early stages of adopting XP, it is possible that the coach would be overloaded while the team learns about the practices, but that would just be a transient start-up situation that would resolve itself in time.

The On-site Customer, working as part of the team, provides other checks and balances. The Release Plan that is produced by the Planning Game balances the value of each incremental release with the costs associated with releasing an updated version to the users. In environments in which the cost of each release is very low and the value of extra functionality is very high, it would be feasible to make a new release every two weeks, whereas in other environments a general release every six months would be too frequent.

Pretty Adventuresome Programming

Although the overdose effect is hard when doing all of the practices, it could be a real hazard for teams that practice what Alistair Cockburn calls "Pretty Adventuresome Programming" [Cockburn, 2000]. Rather than setting the dials on ten, Pretty Adventuresome Programming is *almost* Extreme Programming in that it lacks any rigor about applying the practices. At best this is just using the label XP to cover whatever the development team wants to do at the time. At worst it is a team doing some of the practices some of the time.

Partial compliance with a process is an endemic problem in software development. Sometimes this is an advantage because if the team did not take shortcuts, it would be practically impossible to make any progress. At other times it is very hazardous if the team does only the enjoyable parts of the process or those parts of the process that are easily adopted by the organization. By doing only part of the process, the team exposes itself to lots of potential problems that the full process addressed.

The problem with doing only some of the practices is that the team has to have something in place to prevent their overall approach to software development from becoming unbalanced. With only some of the practices it would be very easy to fall prey to the overdose effect on the practices that the team enjoys doing. For example, Refactoring to achieve a Simple Design is positively hazardous without the safety net provided by the Unit Tests. By simply omitting Test First Development, a team could easily waste a lot of time resolving problems that occur with Continuous Integration that would result from not having a good regression test suite.

The synergistic coupling of the practices in Extreme Programming is an advantage when it comes to ensuring compliance with the process. When all of the practices are being used effectively, XP teams report that their workdays are productive and enjoyable. If the team drifts away from the process, work starts to feel less productive and becomes much less enjoyable. A key job for the coach is to notice the mood of the team, because many XP teams are finding that a decline in enjoyment precedes a decline in measured productivity.

Why Now? What Has Changed?

Many organizations want to get the benefits from a new approach to software development without having to change anything. This happens all of the time and is why it is sometimes necessary to talk about the difference between the espoused process and the actual process. My experience has been that the larger the gap between the espoused process and the actual process, the more stressed the team. Most developers prefer to follow the espoused process and feel uncomfortable when they have to make it up as they go along.

In recent years, the pressure to be more productive has led many organizations to look at alternative approaches to software development. A common problem, however, has been that even though the project team is supposed to use the new approach to be more productive, they were not supposed to stop doing any of their current software development activities. Needless to say, this is not very effective. It also creates a lot of tension for developers because they are never really sure which process they are supposed to be following.

Setting the dials on ten is the way that Extreme Programming talks about the need to ensure that the espoused process is the same as the actual process by rigorously applying all of the practices of XP. Even the name conjures up the idea of commitment and dedication. There is no such thing as half-hearted Extreme Programming.

What Does This Mean for XP?

As with any new approach to software development, there is a real danger that some projects will make a half-hearted attempt to use it, fail, and then attempt to blame the failure on XP. In attempting to mitigate this risk, the XP literature attempts to spell out the need to do all the practices. Unfortunately, in doing so it fails to communicate the need for careful reflection on how a team is practicing XP so that the various practices can be adjusted for local conditions.

The synergistic nature of the practices needs to be communicated better. Currently it is very easy to see the individual practices as simplistic versions of what really needs to be done in software development. The way that the different practices support and reinforce each other does not come across well in most of the XP literature.

Summary

- The synergy between the practices is what makes Extreme Programming different.
- The role of the XP Coach is to ensure that the team stays productive.
- The On-site Customer, working as part of the team, provides other checks and balances.
- Pretty Adventuresome Programming is *almost* Extreme Programming in that it lacks any rigor about applying the practices.
- Partial compliance with a process is an endemic problem in software development.
- Many organizations want to get the benefits from a new approach to software development without having to change anything.
- As with any new approach to software development, there is a real danger that some projects will make a half-hearted attempt to use XP, fail, and then attempt to blame the failure on XP.

Chapter 16

Requirements: Documentation or a Conversation?

At the end of the day, if the software doesn't meet the user's needs, it is still lousy software, regardless of how it was created.

The traditional software engineering approach to software development assumes that requirements are relatively static. As such, it is assumed that requirements can be documented, agreed on, and then signed off with change control procedures put in place to control scope creep on projects.

Unfortunately, the studies that exist suggest that requirements change. Data from Capers Jones suggests that more than one percent of requirements change for every month of project duration [Jones, 1994, p. 93]. No wonder there have to be special practices in place for freezing requirements and controlling scope creep.

In contrast, Extreme Programming projects do not try to produce a detailed requirements document and then freeze it. Instead, the On-site Customer is actively encouraged to steer the project by changing his mind about what exactly it is that the team is supposed to deliver.

Can Changes to Requirements be Controlled?

Yes. There's no question it is possible to control requirements creep such that the development team can deliver the application as originally specified. The big question is whether the resulting application is actually useful. In a way, the idea of freezing requirements is a guarantee that the application that the team delivers is not actually the application that is really wanted.

By freezing requirements, a team is choosing to delay when it recognizes that the requirements have changed. The longer the period of the requirements freeze, the more likely that when the application is eventually delivered it will not match what the users really need. It may, however, still be a reasonable fit, allowing a new project to start to deliver additional functionality while the users happily work with the first version. For most purposes, however, if an application does not meet current requirements it is effectively a buggy application.

Slow-moving environments lend themselves to requirements freezes; fast-moving environments do not. The difference is that between efficiency and effective adaptation. In a nearly static environment, it makes sense to optimize for efficiency, so requirements can be carefully documented and baselined. In a fast-moving, dynamic environment, optimizing for efficiency is completely the wrong strategy; effective adaptation is a much better option. Rather than try to control the changes, we must instead strive to respond rapidly to each change as it occurs.

Requirements Traceability Is One Way to Handle Change

Some projects baseline their requirements documentation and then have a process for recognizing changes as they occur. "Approved" change requests are then periodically released to the development team.

Requirements traceability is the way that this is made to work on really big software engineering projects. As the analysts and designers work on a project, they tag everything with the requirements that generated the item. Careful and painstaking precision is needed in this documentation because it is only really valuable when the requirements traceability is complete. It has to be complete, because the way the work has been divided up, none of the analysts or designers really grasps the overall design. So when an analyst gets a change request, traceability is important to discover which parts of the design, code, and tests need to be modified. On 200+-person teams this is a real issue.

The XP approach to having all requirements be testable and associating the acceptance tests with the user stories provides a relatively easy means of dealing with changing requirements. The changed story is prioritized and assigned to an iteration. During the iteration the acceptance tests are changed to match the changed requirements. These changed tests will now fail and the programming team can then determine what needs to be changed in the overall system.

Can XP really manage to do traceability through acceptance tests?

Does the On-Site Customer Know Enough?

Making requirements a conversation means that both sides need to know enough about how to play their role in the project. Although the programmers on the team can easily learn enough about requirements elicitation to play their part, finding a sufficiently knowledgeable customer can be much harder.

The problem is that the On-site Customer has to have really deep and broad domain knowledge, so that he can explain what is needed, both to the programmers and to the rest of the organization. This depth of knowledge is all too rare. With all the outsourcing, downsizing, and "rightsizing" that has happened in organizations, it can be hard to find people with the requisite depth of knowledge.

At best, the On-site Customer will be able to get the necessary information from their colleagues, but this is likely to slow down the rate of progress. After all, the whole point of having an On-site Customer is so that it is quick and painless for the programmers to get answers to questions. This is definitely not the case when the On-site Customer has to go off and consult with colleagues to get the necessary answers—especially if a meeting is needed to reach consensus between competing views.

Emergent Requirements

A standard joke in the software field is that users never know what they want until you show them something. Then they can figure out what they really want, and it is never what you first showed them. This is not because we do a lousy job of analysis or design, rather it is because each new possibility opens up extra, unforeseen, and unforeseeable opportunities. In other words, new requirements are emergent properties of the application being developed.

The awkward part about emergent requirements is that they emerge through people using the application as part of their normal day. Sure, some new ideas may pop up from prototyping sessions or during testing, but the really interesting emergent requirements show up once the application is in live use.

Dealing with emergent requirements requires an incremental delivery process—one that delivers some functionality and then allows the emergent requirements to get incorporated into the next delivery. Traditionally, software engineering has resisted these types of emergent requirements, labeling them *scope creep*. More incremental development processes have used this to improve the software rapidly with each succeeding release.

Why Now? What Has Changed?

Adaptation and the increasing speed of change has become important for many businesses. They want to be able to respond to competitors and opportunities faster than they have typically done in the past. The old way of completely documenting all of the requirements before starting development puts too much delay into the process for many organizations. They need a way to get started with partial requirements so that they can respond quicker.

Flexibility is also key because organizations perceive that they need to be able to respond faster to changes. By working incrementally and using verbal requirements, organizations have been able to become more responsive, but managers have had to get used to a different set of controls on projects.

What Does This Mean for XP?

The On-site Customer role is a very demanding one. Indeed, Chet Hendrickson, a coauthor of *Extreme Programming Installed* [Jeffries, 2001], asked the question, "Can you do everything that is required to be an XP customer and remain healthy?" in a workshop held at OOP-SLA 2001. Much more work needs to be done to help the individuals in the role of On-site Customer learn how to do the job while working at a Sustainable Pace. The way that the On-Site Customer role is now explained suggests that this is not really a job for an individual, rather it is a role that should be fulfilled by a small team of domain experts, testers, and systems analysts.

Maybe Extreme Programming needs to look to the other Agile Methods for other ways of managing incremental requirements capture [http://www.xprogramming.com/xpmag/incremental_req1.htm]. While it would be good not to lose the flexibility offered by the current approach, the reliance on deep domain knowledge limits the applicability of XP. For some complex domains, business analysts are necessary to uncover the underlying requirements and business rules. There is literally nobody in the organization who knows enough to undertake the On-site Customer role effectively.

Summary

- ✧ The traditional software engineering approach to software development assumes that requirements are relatively static.
- ✧ In XP, the On-site Customer is actively encouraged to steer the project by changing his mind about what exactly it is that the team is supposed to deliver.
- ✧ Teams that have a requirements freeze are choosing to delay when changes to requirements will be recognized.
- ✧ Slow-moving environments lend themselves to requirements freezes; fast-moving environments do not.
- ✧ Finding a sufficiently knowledgeable person to fill the role of on-site customer can be hard.
- ✧ Some XP teams are finding that it is possible to have systems analysts assist the On-site Customer in defining the user stories and creating acceptance tests.

Chapter 17

Is Oral Documentation Enough?

Reading is not the same as knowing.

Historically, in traditional software engineering teams, everything was written down and clearly documented, with all documentation being subject to reviews to ensure that it was complete and correct. In practice, on many projects what happens is that this design documentation is never really kept up to date, so most developers learn not to trust the documentation and prefer to read the source code. Unfortunately, the source code is typically written without much understanding of the overall design, so it is hard for maintenance programmers to really figure out the overall system from the code.

The XP focus on using the source code as the primary documentation for the system is similar in many ways to the literate programming style [http://www.literateprogramming.com/] of writing code. In literate programming, the idea is that the source and documentation can be combined into a single source document so that appropriate documentation can be generated from the source. In Extreme Programming, the idea is to write intention-revealing code so that additional comments are no longer necessary. The code should express the intentions of the overall design so that reading the code is a feasible way of understanding the overall system.

Extreme Programming is not, however, averse to documentation. It does, however, challenge the value and utility of much of the documentation that other approaches require. With XP, the goal is only to write documentation when there is a definite, expressed need, and then to raise the quality of the resulting document so that it stands out as an example of good technical writing. This stance ensures that the documentation that is written is both valuable and readable.

Who Reads the Documentation?

A key question to ask is who needs this documentation? Who is going to read it and for what purpose? With the traditional approach there are many handoffs of information from one team to another, so a formal written record of the information is necessary. The recipient is expected to read the documents to gather necessary information and to ask only clarifying questions if the necessary information is not in the documentation.

In Extreme Programming, there are very few handoffs from one person to another. Because information rarely needs to be handed off, XP can rely on oral tradition, clean code, and unit tests to remember most of the design details. After all, the whole point of the Simple Design and the System Metaphor practices is to make sure the software is understandable to the entire team. When extra information is needed, a short technical memo can be used to document the rationale behind various design decisions.

Within an XP team there is very little need for design documentation because nobody needs to read it. Team members either remember the information or can ask another team member. The question of "What happens if we forget?" just does not show up in an oral culture, because if it is important it will be remembered and, by implication, if it is forgotten it was obviously not important.

This is in stark contrast to traditional projects, which are based around writing. Everything has to be written down because writing is the primary means of communication. Forgetting some information is not allowed and is prevented by making sure that everything gets written down. From this viewpoint, XP projects have woefully inadequate documentation because from a literate culture standpoint, an oral tradition is a completely inadequate means of remembering information.

In the debates that have raged between these two viewpoints, one aspect that has been overlooked is the difference between design documentation and usage documentation. The key distinction is that not all documentation is created equally. Usage documentation, things like user guides, on-line help, and API documentation, is going to be read by people outside the development team and is an important project deliverable. Design documentation, things like UML models, program specifications, and meeting minutes, is written to assist the team in creating and delivering the application. This internal documentation is important only if the process requires it. The fact that a process does or does not produce a certain item of documentation says nothing about the value or usefulness of the process.

Is a Handoff to Maintenance Useful?

XP and the traditional approaches to software development really come into conflict when we consider what happens after the team has successfully delivered the application. With the traditional approach there is the assumption that the documentation will be handed over to the maintenance team, and the original development team can move on to other projects. Because XP does not have any real documentation that could be passed over to the maintenance team, it is obviously a defective process.

The interesting thing about XP, however, is that it assumes that applications are never really going to be handed off to a separate maintenance team. The assumption is that after each incremental release, the customer will want more functionality and keep funding the development team. There is an expectation that, over time, the size of the development team will be scaled back, but it assumes that the organization will have a near-continuous stream of enhancements and change requests. As such, there is never a need to hand the application over to a maintenance team; the original development team can continue to support the application indefinitely.

The expectation on XP projects is that there will be sufficient time allowed for transition when new team members are brought in to replace existing team members. Hence, it is feasible to replace the entire team, but it has to happen slowly in order to preserve the oral tradition. If it has to happen quickly, then the On-site Customer is expected to schedule the creation of maintenance documentation just like any other User Story. It is doubtful, in practice, if this would actually happen.

Can Maintainers Really Rely on the Documentation?

Before we write off XP because of the lack of documentation, we need to look at what maintenance programmers actually do when faced with a new application. Yes, they will attempt to read the documentation if it exists, but what if there are several thousand pages of analysis notes, design documents, and program specifications? At best they will only skim through the documentation.

What they will usually do is talk to the original team members if they can, chat with the users, and play around on the test system to figure out how the application works. They will also poke around at the code and figure out how to build the application.

When they do get a bug to fix, maintenance programmers are generally very skeptical about the documentation, assuming that, over time, the code has probably drifted away from the design as written down. In part, this is because they know that with the constant pressure to fix bugs and get the updated system released, they rarely have time to go back through all the documentation and fix it to match the changed system. The better maintenance programmers know that even the comments in the code will, in all probability, be incorrect because in the heat of the moment it is all too easy to change the code and forget to fix the comments.

Eventually what happens is that the maintenance team builds up an oral tradition around each application it maintains. The better ones build up a minimal set of reliable documentation for each application, and although it may be more than what an XP team would produce, it is always less than what would have been handed over from a traditional software engineering team. After all, when it comes down to it, a maintenance programmer becomes really effective only when he has learned the application and is familiar with the code.

With Extreme Programming, however, the maintenance team can rely on one form of documentation that is guaranteed to be up to date—the test suite. The unit tests are a great starting point for understanding what every method of every class is supposed to be doing. Similarly, the acceptance tests are a great place to find out what the overall application is supposed to do. As long as the maintenance team practices Test First Development, they ensure that this "documentation" is always kept up to date.

The big question, of course, is whether the maintenance team will practice Test First Development. My experience has been that few maintenance teams keep the documentation up to date with their changes to an application, so unless there is an XP coach in place to support the maintenance team, it is very unlikely that the test suite will be kept up to date.

Why Now? What Has Changed?

Organizations are starting to realize that system complexity has risen to the point whereby a simple handoff of documentation to maintenance is not really feasible. For large systems, some of the original development team have to stay around to support the application until over time, the maintenance developers can learn the overall system.

At the same time, however, some organizations like the idea of outsourcing both the development and maintenance of applications. Interestingly, organizations are also starting to realize that there is a very large amount of intellectual capital tied up in the heads of the original developers. As a result, there is a demand for clean, well-written code that is easier to understand, which partially explains why books on Refactoring [Fowler, 1999] have become so popular.

What Does This Mean for XP?

Oral documentation means that XP does not really support the idea of handing an application off to the maintenance team. While personally I think this is actually a step forward, it is contrary to the way that many organizations have their maintenance departments set up. To work around this, before disbanding an XP project team, it would be useful to have the maintenance team work with the project team on the last few iterations so that they get familiar with the code.

Alternatively, the On-site Customer must schedule some user stories that request maintenance documentation that explains the overall design, before they disband the team. Otherwise the maintenance team will face several months of confusion as they try to understand the application. In a way this could be seen as a hidden cost of using XP—a continuous thread of active staff to maintain the oral knowledge about the code costs real money. Disbanding an XP team without getting the team members to document the internals of the application would be unwise, but this documentation, written right at the end of a project, although it would represent the finished design, is unlikely to be of high quality. Indeed, it would probably fall prey to many of the ills of traditional documentation and it is very unlikely that future maintenance programmers would trust it.

If XP applications are handed off to a maintenance team, that team is going to have to be trained to use XP if the new application is expected to stay maintainable. The reason is that the unit and acceptance tests have to be kept up to date with the application. Several times now I have heard of programmers who are unfamiliar with Test First Development actually deleting failing tests, because they are convinced their code is correct and the test is at fault, only to see the application fail in production several months later. In addition, if new functionality is added without adding extra tests, then the fact that all tests pass is giving a false sense of security about the quality of all the code.

Summary

⋄ In practice, traditional design documentation is rarely kept up to date, so most developers learn not to trust the documentation and prefer to read the source code.

⋄ The fact that a process does or does not produce a certain item of documentation says nothing about the value or usefulness of the process.

⋄ XP assumes that applications are never really going to be handed off to a separate maintenance team.

⋄ Eventually maintenance teams build up an oral tradition around every application.

⋄ Organizations are starting to realize that system complexity has risen to the point whereby a simple handoff of documentation to maintenance is not really feasible.

Chapter 18

Playing to Win?

I'm not competitive. I just win.

Extreme Programming is a reaction to the idea that following a process is an acceptable way of failing. As Beck states, "Everyone is trying to develop 'by the book,' not because it makes any particular sense, but because they want to be able to say at the end that it wasn't their fault, they were following the process." [Beck, 2000, p. 40] The idea behind playing to win is to do everything that helps the team win and to avoid doing anything that does not contribute to that goal.

The obvious question, though, is whether playing to win exposes the project to additional downside risks. After all, playing to win is a reasonable strategy only if there is a large upside for a win and little downside for a loss. Playing to win is a good idea for sports teams, because losing a game does not have serious consequences. Over the course of a complete season the strategy might pay off, but even if it doesn't, the fans will be entertained by the wide-open play. Losing the game isn't really a big deal if the fans can see that their team is going all out for a win.

Can the same be said of a software development team? Will the managers and users applaud a failed project and give the team another chance? Not in my experience. After any failed project there is nearly always a witch hunt that ends up assigning blame to someone. So for most software development projects there is a large downside to failing. As such, playing to win, although a good sound bite, could be thought of as an unwise option if it were not for the fact that morale and motivation play such a large part of success in projects.

- -

In my experience, from all the projects I've visited over the years, demotivated, demoralized teams don't seem to deliver successfully. These are rarely teams that have been allowed to choose their own process; mostly they are (reluctantly) following whatever process they are required to use. Allowing a team to choose their own process changes the morale and motivation and, in this context "playing to win" makes sense. After all, the team is going to choose the process that gives them the best chance of success and they will want to make a success of "their" process.

Does XP Actively Manage All Risks?

Does playing to win mean actively managing all project risks or does XP ignore some risks, trusting that the team will do the right thing? Looking in detail at the practices, it appears that XP follows the second strategy. It does not attempt to manage all risks, choosing instead to monitor continually the progress of the project. Whenever the project indicators suggest something is going wrong, the team has to steer the project back in the right direction.

The underlying world view is that a disaster will not happen. Sure, there may be a few bumps along the way, but basically everything will turn out OK. Depending on your point of view, this is either seeing the world through rose-tinted glasses or a reasonably pragmatic stance.

By choosing to ignore some risks until they actually arise, XP projects are able to proceed faster, but they leave themselves open to accusations of recklessness and hacking. Because XP assumes an amicable relationship between the programmers and the On-site Customer, there is very little written down to substantiate the work that has been requested. Yes, there are always the User Stories, but I can imagine problems trying to sort out what went wrong when all that remains is a stack of story cards.

So, is this aspect of playing to win a realistic strategy for most organizations and projects? Probably not in most cases. True, high-profile projects could probably get away with it, as could projects that are in the process of being "rescued from imminent failure." But, for many organizations, neglecting obvious risks rates as a career-limiting move in most cases.

Does XP Require Experienced Teams?

Playing to win assumes that the team will do the right thing rather than follow the book. As such, the amount of detailed guidance given in the XP literature is much lower than in other methodologies. The team is supposed to reflect actively on their process and tune the practices as needed. To be successful at this, however, at least a third of the team must be experienced software developers.

Yes, I have heard claims of success with talented but inexperienced teams, but that does not mean that you would want to try that strategy. True, the Pair Programming and collaborative development aspects of XP make XP projects a good learning environment for inexperienced developers, but just because you can, doesn't mean that you should. After all, if you are serious about playing to win, you will always want to balance the enthusiasm and talent of beginners with seasoned, experienced developers.

Can We Win With a Team of Novices?

Although this may theoretically be possible, I have to question the sanity of any organization that would assemble a team of novices and then claim that it is playing to win. There is a subtle mismatch between word and deed.

Regardless of the software development approach selected, a team of novices is going to struggle and have a much lower probability of success than a more experienced team. An experienced coach might be able to mitigate the worst of the risks for a small team of novices, such that they quickly learn from their mistakes, but my guess is that it would be better to have the coach take a month or two to train the novices before starting the project.

Yes, you could plausibly suggest that the collaborative practices of XP would allow a team of novices to learn faster than in a traditional team of novices, but that avoids the question of why use a team of novices in the first place. Low-experience teams are hazardous to the health of any project, especially if the team members are convinced that because they know objects, design patterns, UML, and Java they are bound to be successful. Knowledge of these things helps, but there is a lot more to a successful software development team than a bunch of individuals who happen to know some esoteric technology.

Why Now? What Has Changed?

There is a lot of pressure to get applications shipped in shorter and shorter timescales. Using the same process that was used in the past isn't a realistic way of drastically compressing a schedule. A different process is required. Extreme Programming is an uncompromising approach to software development that throws down a challenge that states that, if the project really is important, demonstrate it by assigning a full-time, On-site Customer to assist the team.

By taking everything to extremes, XP is a deliberate attempt to step productivity up to the next level. The practices force the team to really focus on delivering the most important parts of the application, as judged by the empowered On-site Customer.

What Does This Mean for XP?

Although *playing to win* is a nice sound bite, it can come across as a very divisive expression. It immediately sets up the opposite, *playing to lose,* and in so doing implies that all other software development processes are inferior. Although this may be a good advertising strategy for some things, the undertone of world domination has meant that it has generated some hostility toward XP.

Playing to win can also be a losing proposition in some organizations because it leaves the team too exposed to criticism. In the usual jockeying for funding between departments, it would be all too easy for doubts to be cast about how well an XP project is handling potential risks. Yes, the XP team could counter by showing their record of regular releases, but an XP project is not immune to political maneuvering. To counter this you would probably be advised to ensure that you have support for Extreme Programming at the highest levels before embarking on your first XP project.

Summary

- ✧ Extreme Programming is a reaction to the idea that following a process is an acceptable way of failing.
- ✧ By choosing to ignore some risks until they actually arise, XP projects are able to proceed faster, but they leave themselves open to accusations of recklessness and hacking.

- ✧ I have to question the sanity of any organization that would assemble a team of novices for use on an XP project.
- ✧ Regardless of the software development approach selected, a team of novices is going to struggle and have a much lower probability of success than a more experienced team.
- ✧ There is a lot of pressure to get applications shipped in shorter and shorter timescales.
- ✧ XP is a deliberate attempt to step productivity up to the next level.

Part V

Understanding the XP Community

Software developers are a strange bunch.

From the outside, the XP community is really hard to understand and come to grips with. A very visible part is the fervor with which proponents of XP act as really passionate evangelists for this new approach to software development. Indeed, many come across as zealots that have been brainwashed into the XP cult.

In part, this is understandable because it is strange to see software developers get really passionate about anything. For better or worse, XP projects are actually fun to work on, and that is sure worth talking about. Unfortunately, many proponents choose to describe XP in terms that are derogatory toward other approaches to software development. While the resulting controversy can be useful for attracting attention in the long run, it makes it much harder for XP to move into the mainstream of software development.

Another interesting barrier to understanding XP is the way that the XP community has built up a jargon of its own. Part of the problem is that a lot of the original ideas for XP were written up on a Wiki Web [Leuf, 2001], and the way that pages are named on a Wiki Web has resulted in some ReallyStrangeSayings.

The other part of understanding the XP community involves looking at where XP fits with all the other approaches to software development. Right now, XP practitioners are focused on finding ways to transition projects to XP, but for me, the real question is how do projects transition away from XP?

Chapter 19

ReallyStrangeSayings

Every field of human endeavor has its own jargon, but programmers seem to take pride in making the jargon incomprehensible.

An essential part of understanding Extreme Programming involves learning the jargon. This can be a rather daunting task because the XP community seems to have its own rules for making up words to represent many core ideas.

Ward Cunningham's Wiki Web software has a lot to answer for [Leuf, 2001]. By enabling collaborative writing on the Web, it provided a mechanism for Extreme Programming ideas to be both refined and publicized. At the same time, the way the Wiki Web software uses Mixed-Case WikiWords [`http://c2.com/cgi-bin/wiki?WikiWords`] to identify links has led to some really strange jargon in the XP community.

MixedCase and Initial-Slang

Although the practices that have evolved into XP have been around for a long time, the current formulation was refined in the period from 1998 to 2000. During this period, many of the various sayings in the XP community were posted on a Wiki Web, so an appropriate WikiWord was created. In practice, some of these were very long to type, so in time the longer WikiWords were just referred to by an initial-slang version of the WikiWord.

An example of this is the contraction of YouArentGonnaNeedIt [`http://c2.com/cgi-bin/wiki?YouArentGonnaNeedIt`] to YAGNI. In XP, deferring adding of features until they are actually needed is such a central theme that the contraction was natural. For the same reason, OnceAndOnlyOnce contracted to OAOO, and BigDesignUpFront contracted to BDUF.

WikiWords Are Not Always Politically Correct

One very interesting thing that can happen in an on-line community is that what gets written down is a provocative formulation of an idea. When it comes to expressing ideas, *better raw than wrong* is the strategy of choice [Pavlicek, 2000, p. 75]. What gets written down is the essence of what distinguishes the idea from other ideas and it is easy, when reading without knowing the rest of the context, for the reader to be surprised by the bluntness of the words. This is also compounded by the way that the XP community has sought to distinguish itself from other approaches to software development.

For example, although XP puts a lot of emphasis on the design activity, it is easy when reading the words around BigDesignUpFront (BDUF) to come away with the impression that XP does not value or practice design. In reality, many of the XP practices are explicitly about how to do design XP style. But all the same, it is very easy to come away with the impression that BDUF is an unworkable strategy for software development.

The important thing to remember when looking at any XP literature is that, to a large extent, what has been written is there to make it really clear that XP is distinct from other approaches. At first this was necessary to establish a distinct identity for XP, and more recently it has been necessary to distinguish XP from Pretty Adventuresome Programming.

YouAren'tGonnaNeedIt

YAGNI is an early formulation of the Simple Design practice in XP. It evolved from the fear that developers would add unnecessary features. It is a direct response to claims that "we are going to need this when ..."—"You aren't gonna need it."

This is difficult to understand from the viewpoint of change being expensive, because that mind-set assumes that adding features later will cost more. From the viewpoint of change being cheap, however, adding features later is better because that mind-set assumes that unnecessary features are expensive extra baggage that has to be carried.

Resolving the tension between these two viewpoints is key to understanding Extreme Programming. In XP it is the On-site Customer who gets to specify the features that are needed. Any feature that is not needed to support the current set of tests is obviously unnecessary. This prevents the debate that can otherwise occur about which potential future features should be designed in at the start.

The Source Code Is the Design

Jack Reeves' article "What is Software Design?" [Reeves, 1992] has been very influential in shaping ideas in the XP community about documentation. The basic idea is that source code can be very readable, so there is little value in producing higher-level descriptions of the design unless they are short enough to be readable.

The issue is that although it can be easy to communicate high-level design ideas, the technical team is going to have to understand the real design details. Problems start to arise when the design documents get to be really voluminous. At some point the documentation is so large and complex it might actually be easier to read the source. Martin Fowler [Fowler, 1997] talked about this in an article called "The Almighty Thud," when he points out that the goal behind the documentation is communication. If we really need the intricate details, we can go to the code. What we need are short, concise descriptions of the "key aspects of the system that, once understood, will help someone to learn more."

Obviously, the idea behind the source code is the design works only if the designer also does the programming. In all other cases, a lot of intermediate design documentation has to be created to pass the ideas from the designer to the programmers.

OnceAndOnlyOnce

OAOO is another part of Simple Design. It is a warning against the common practice of copy-and-paste programming in which developers copy large chunks of code and duplicate the functionality throughout the program. Although this quick-and-dirty technique can be useful for getting something to run, the resulting duplication makes programs very hard to evolve and maintain.

Sometimes the debates about potentially hidden duplication violating OAOO can seem like the medieval debates about how many angels can dance on the head of a pin. Indeed, it can sometimes seem that the XP community sees duplication as an evil that must be rooted out wherever it can be found. In practice, however, there is a fairly well recognized set of code smells [Fowler, 1999, p. 75–88] that indicate that refactoring is necessary.

Interestingly, there is another, simpler formulation of OAOO in *The Pragmatic Programmer:* Don't Repeat Yourself (DRY) [Hunt, 2000, p. 27]. In a sense, OAOO is too limiting a concept because, as the DRY principle states, "Every piece of knowledge must have a single, unambiguous, authoritative representation within a system." In this formulation, the debates about documentation disappear. You only have to document the stuff that isn't already expressed in the code.

Do the Simplest Thing That Could Possibly Work

This saying, often abbreviated to DTSTTCPW, is yet another reminder to follow the Simple Design practice. The idea is to find the simplest code that can add the new functionality you need. At one point in the evolution of Extreme Programming there was even the suggestion that design sessions should be limited to less than 15 minutes before the ideas should be tested out by writing code.

There is, however, a problem with this saying. Just what exactly is "the simplest thing" and when does "the simplest thing" become "the stupidest thing?" The experience of the developers affects this, because a developer who is not very familiar with a relational database could easily consider storing data in flat files to be a "simpler" solution. In the same vein, another developer could easily argue for using a relational database because it is much easier to search for records in a database than it is in a flat file. After all, the database engine code has already been written.

As with all ideas in Extreme Programming, the solution to this dilemma is not to get hung up in debates about what "simplest" really means, but to focus on the intention behind the idea. Many projects have gotten into trouble in the past because the developers have tried to build a completely general, optimal solution. Indeed, a common joke is that some programmers would rather build an application generator (and use it to build the application) rather than simply build the application. Most of the time this is an obvious case of what Kent Beck

[Beck, 2000] called *false feature rich*, and the obvious solution is to ask the developer to do the simplest thing that could possibly work.

The real problem is that the idea of building generic, optimal solutions is really seductive. After all, what could be more effective than writing a simple report generator and using it to produce the reports? It will obviously be much faster than having to develop 20 different reports. Unfortunately, it is never that simple. All too many projects have wasted lots of time and money building a simple bit of generic infrastructure, so to address this risk Extreme Programming has an explicit saying to warn against this mistake.

Getting Beyond the Sayings

Most of the recent material written about Extreme Programming is relatively accessible. It is mainly the older, on-line material that tends to be rather cryptic and hard to understand. Although the rhetoric surrounding XP is starting to moderate, the assumptions and worldview of Extreme Programming are still widely separate from the assumptions and worldview of mainstream software engineering.

When trying to understand the XP literature, you may find it useful to assume temporarily that the ideas do actually work. By actively suspending disbelief for a short time, you may find it easier to understand what has been written, even though you know that the ideas would not work in your own environment.

All the practices in Extreme Programming are synergistic and situational. This means that outside the context of an XP project, a practice or saying may appear to be less than optimal advice. Within the context of an XP project, however, the advice is sound, even though it may not match the advice that would be given in any other software development process.

In the end, the sayings are really intended for use by the XP Coach as a shorthand way of reminding an XP team about what needs to be done to stay on process. Outside the context of a coaching conversation with individuals in an XP team, these sayings can be really confusing. After reminding one programmer to do the simplest thing, an XP Coach could easily remind another that a relatively complex Design Pattern [Gamma, 1995] would restore the balance of OAOO.

Summary

◇ An essential part of understanding Extreme Programming involves learning the jargon.

◇ One very interesting thing that can happen in an on-line community is that what gets written down is a provocative formulation of an idea.

◇ To a large extent the XP literature highlights what is different about XP; the common aspects are downplayed.

◇ All the practices in Extreme Programming are synergistic and situational. This means that outside the context of an XP project, a practice or saying may appear to be less than optimal advice.

◇ Outside the context of a coaching conversation with individuals in an XP team, many XP sayings can be really confusing.

Chapter 20

Feel the Hostility;
Experience the Joy

When will flame wars become an Olympic sport?

There is a drastic disconnect between the XP community and parts of the software engineering community. In part, this disconnect has been deliberately created as a means of distinguishing XP from all the other approaches to software development, but that is not the only reason. XP does directly challenge some of the sacred cows of the software engineering community. By elevating the status of the programmer, it is turning nearly 30 years of software engineering orthodoxy upside-down.

Just a Bunch of Undisciplined Hacker Cowboys?

A very common charge that is laid against XP is that it is just undisciplined hacking. This charge is an easy one because XP does encourage coding to start before all the requirements are well understood and before all of the design is completed. For some, this is direct evidence that XP is encouraging the bad practices from the old days when programmers would just sit down and code stuff without really understanding what they were doing.

If any further evidence was needed to convict the cowboys, all you need to do is hear the jokes around BDUF and the UML "It is OK to write UML diagrams, just wash your hands afterward." Sounds really bad doesn't it? It sure does until you understand that some XP teams use whiteboards to sketch out design ideas, and as anyone who has ever used a whiteboard knows, your hands get dirty quite quickly from using the whiteboard pens.

In contrast to the accusation of being undisciplined cowboys, XP is in fact a very disciplined, collaborative approach to software development. Admittedly it is a very different discipline than you would expect on a high-ceremony software engineering project, but it is still very disciplined.

As for the charge that XP "encourages coding to start before all the requirements are well understood and before all of the design is completed"—that is a defining characteristic of all incremental development processes. Even the Unified Process practices incremental requirements capture, which means that code is written before all of the requirements are well understood or even documented. XP, however, has the image problem because it follows Tom Gilb's advice and uses short, two- or three-week delivery cycles [Gilb, 1988], which makes the incremental requirements capture really obvious.

Is XP a Return to the Dark Ages?

Another common accusation laid against XP is that it is ignoring the wisdom and experience that has built up in the software engineering community over the last 30 years. Evidence for this abounds. Requirements are not traceable, formal inspections and reviews are not performed, practically nothing gets documented, there is no real domain analysis, the overall system architecture is not designed before coding starts, programmers are testing their own code, and any technical person who does not write code is ridiculed! Case closed.

Interestingly, though, Linus Torvalds wrote the following when discussing the design of Linux on November 30, 2001:

> . . . I will go further and claim that _no_ major software project that has been successful in a general marketplace (as opposed to niches) has ever gone through those nice lifecycles they tell you about in CompSci classes. Have you _ever_ heard of a project that actually started off with trying to figure out what it should do, a rigorous design phase, and a implementation phase?
> Dream on.
> Software evolves. It isn't designed. The only question is how strictly you _control_ the evolution, and how open you are to external sources of mutations. ["Linus Says: Linux Not Designed; It Never Was" http://kerneltrap.org/article.php?sid=398]

You could make the claim that what Extreme Programming is doing is bringing the practices that have been used very successfully for *software product development* into the mainstream. It attempts to implement the maximum number of useful, valuable features in minimum calendar time, and it does this by focusing on adding feature by feature. For commercial software products, doing up-front analysis and design for a feature that is never delivered is a serious cost. By avoiding doing analysis and design for features that will never make the grade, it is possible to add other, more useful features.

The Best Project We Have Ever Worked On!

In contrast to the hostility expressed by parts of the software engineering community, programmers who have been members of successful XP teams never want to go back to working the old way. Most are converted into evangelists for the XP way. Some become really zealous converts and end up hyping and overpromoting the potential benefits and applicability of Extreme Programming.

This can lead to really strange conversations that are vaguely reminiscent of 1960's-type conversations: "You shouldn't knock it until you have tried it." The underlying premise is that XP is so different it is practically impossible to explain; it has to be experienced. If you would just open your mind and actually work as part of an XP team, you would see the light.

The gulf between the zealots and the detractors is so wide that it will take a long time before a truce is called in the ongoing flame wars. The problem is that, taken individually, many of the practices in XP are very reminiscent of the haphazard approaches to software development that made software engineering a necessity. The idea that a synergistic combination of unsafe practices could actually give a useful outcome continues to fuel the debates.

Developers Are Attracted to XP

There are two things that really strike me about developers who use Extreme Programming:

1. They really like programming
2. They really like working on XP projects

Although these observations could be dismissed as being obvious, that would be a mistake because they reveal an interesting aspect of Extreme Programming—the fact that XP considers *developer enjoyment of the process* important.

No wonder, then, that developers are attracted to Extreme Programming. It values what developers consider to be important. It allows developers to get involved in all aspects of a project, and enables every developer on the team to gain a broad knowledge of the overall application. Indeed, it could be said that XP encourages developers to gain deep knowledge about the entire application.

Extreme Programming also taps into the pride in work that most developers share. At least half the practices are intended to address code quality and maintainability: pair programming, refactoring, collective ownership, coding standards, simple design, system metaphor, and unit tests. Couple this with iterative development leading to small releases so that developers can see their code going into production and it is easy to see why developers are attracted to Extreme Programming.

So Is XP a Cult?

No, but it has definitely tapped into the psyche of some programmers. It just seems to resonate and feel right.

XP is very appealing to programmers because it lets them do what they really like to do—write programs. It includes just enough checks and balances to make sure that a small team of programmers can successfully deliver useful applications while enjoying what they like to do best.

Small wonder, then, that programmers who are members of successful XP teams are practically zealots out to convert the world to Extreme Programming. It is also no surprise that when these zealots talk to the reactionary old guard software engineers, sparks begin to fly. Neither can really communicate with the other because there is no real shared experience or common ground.

Programmers who really like to program are not really attracted to software engineering, and software engineers are not usually very passionate about writing programs. Add to this the fact that Extreme Programming arose in the software development community, whereas software engineering has very strong roots in the academic community, and it is really easy to see why Extreme Programming is so controversial. The accusation that XP is a cult is just one sign that in the desire to promote their "breakthrough," the originators of XP did not do the studies required to convince the academics in the software engineering community of the validity of the new approach.

Summary

⬦ The claim that XP is just undisciplined hacking is an easy one to make.

⬦ In reality, XP is an extremely disciplined approach to software development.

⬦ Extreme Programming is bringing the practices that have been used very successfully for software product development into the mainstream.

⬦ Programmers who have been members of successful XP teams never want to go back to working the old way. Most are converted into evangelists for the XP way.

⬦ XP is very appealing to programmers because it lets them do what they really like to do—write programs.

⬦ The fact that many see Extreme Programming as an alternative to software engineering is yet more fuel for the raging controversy.

Chapter 21

Transitioning Away From Extreme Programming

Wouldn't it be great if there was a software development process that systems analysts raved about?

Currently the XP community is focused closely on the problems of adopting XP, but a more interesting question is, how do you transition away from Extreme Programming?

This is an interesting question, because XP is very appealing to programmers but is not suitable for all kinds of projects. Yes, it may be feasible to restructure your organization and projects to make them more suitable and amenable to Extreme Programming, but for some projects you may have to find an alternative process. In doing so, you are likely to face resistance from your XP teams because the sense of control over their work that Extreme Programming gives is very addictive. Very few people who have worked as part of a well-functioning XP team have expressed any interest in using a different process.

But Extreme Programming is not the last word in software development processes. Eventually it will be superseded by another process, and even in organizations that have fully adopted XP, some projects will need a different process. So, how does an organization go about switching from Extreme Programming to a different approach to software development?

Does XP Lock a Project into the Extreme Practices?

Possibly. The problem is that XP generates few of the deliverables that are expected by other approaches to software development. As such, it would be very hard for a traditional software engineering team to maintain an application developed using XP because there would be few analysis and design artifacts. Although it might be possible for the outgoing XP team to generate the necessary documentation, in practice this could prove to be difficult, especially if the XP team members are not familiar with UML and similar documentation standards.

The maintenance team could just take over the code and then try to reverse engineer the design details from the code, but this would not recover the missing requirements documentation. It would also require a dramatic improvement in the capabilities of reverse engineering tools. Although it is possible to generate UML diagrams from source code, the resulting diagrams are not always very readable.

Interestingly, even though few traditional maintenance teams actually trust the documentation, they still expect to be given the documentation. As such, applications produced by XP teams would be seen as deficient in that the expected models and documentation would not exist.

Of course, it is possible to make the claim that the code inherited from an XP team would be much simpler and easier to understand than code from other approaches, but that does not get around the problem that reading code takes a lot of effort. Although the programmers can do this, systems analysts and designers will have very little to guide them in understanding the application.

Welcome to the Hotel California?

Yes, you can check out but you can never leave. Some programmers really like using XP, and do not want to go back to the old way of developing software. Often they do not want to try any other new way either. Having found a programmer's nirvana in XP, they just do not want to leave. Programmers really value the sense of control and accomplishment that comes with Extreme Programming. Let's face it. People become software developers because they want to write software and, in XP projects, the programmers get to write software most days. Every couple of weeks the team gets to celebrate shipping some valuable functionality.

The sense of accomplishment that comes from delivering value means that whatever process you want to use instead of XP has to have a really compelling story for the developers. After all, historically software developers have had a raw deal from most software development processes. Often there has been the feeling that the process hasn't made it possible to deliver the kind of quality code that they feel they should be delivering. In contrast, XP allows them to write code that they are proud to show to their teammates.

This is going to be a real challenge to methodologists in the future: how to create a new approach to software development that is as compelling for the programmers as XP. *"This is the best project we have ever worked on"* is a really tough act to follow.

Retraining Extreme Programmers

Assuming for a moment that Extreme Programming is going to continue to grow in popularity and be used on more projects, eventually we could get to the stage when there are some software developers who have only ever worked on XP projects. At that point we will face the situation of having to retrain XP team members in alternative approaches to software development. This will probably be just as much a culture shock as it has been for mainframe programmers getting retrained in object-oriented programming and client/server development.

Moving from the emergent requirements paradigm of XP to a more formal documented requirements and design paradigm will be a real challenge. Instead of allowing the design to emerge through test first development and refactoring, programmers will be expected to write code from a detailed specification. In addition, some will be expected to stop programming and learn to do just analysis and design. That is likely to be a really hard transition.

Retraining Customers

I expect that transitioning the On-site Customer away from Extreme Programming is likely to prove difficult. Once someone is used to being able to steer the project and get a new release every two or three weeks, it will be a real shock to go back to the old ways. Instead of being completely involved in the development process, the customer will be expected to talk to the systems analysts and explain what is needed. After that conversation has been recorded, interpreted, and passed on to the designer, the customer will probably find that what the programmer has been asked to do bears no real relationship to what was originally asked for. Even worse, rather than getting a new release every two or three weeks, the customer will be lucky to get a release every two or three months.

The customers might be pleasantly surprised to find that there are dedicated testing resources allocated to assist with the testing, but they will be horrified by how late it occurs in the development cycle.

There will probably also be a lot of stress associated with change requests. After all, the On-site Customer will be used to having the XP team run the Planning Game to slot the new functionality into the appropriate place in the schedule. The concept of frozen requirements and negotiating for change requests is going to seem very strange and stilted. The customer is very likely to say, "And this is supposed to give me better applications?"

What Is Next After Extreme Programming?

Although you could easily be misled into thinking that XP is the ultimate approach to software development, there are many competing approaches out there. Sooner or later another approach will catch the attention of the software development community and XP will become just another way to develop software. Personally, I think that this cannot happen soon enough, because the hype surrounding Extreme Programming hinders reasonable discussions about where it works and how to apply it.

Obviously, there will be many attempts at creating hybrids based on Extreme Programming, in an attempt to extend into areas not currently covered by XP. One such example is Mike Beedle's XBreed [http:// www.xbreed.net/], which is a hybrid of XP and Scrum, which extends the ideas of XP into developing multiple applications and shared components. XBreed uses Scrum to coordinate between the teams, with XP used within each team. Many other groups are experimenting with a form of "distributed" XP, in which the team is not colocated and uses various electronic presence technologies for communication within the team.

The software engineering community will also be a source of interesting approaches once the idea of "Executable UML" takes hold. This will be interesting to watch because it will be promoted by the tool vendors and standards organizations, whereas Extreme Programming was practically a grassroots movement.

Overall, though, any successor or alternative to XP will have to be superlative to supplant it in teams that have a lot of experience in using XP. This is not to say that XP is the end of the line for process evolution, just that XP is very captivating for a lot of people. It is a development process that people actually enjoy using.

Where Will the Next Process Come From?

The success of Extreme Programming has reawakened interest in software development methodologies. The fact that it has become popular without large organizational backing or promoting represents a large shift in the software development community.

The grassroots nature of Extreme Programming means that developers can no longer idly complain about the stupidity of their methodology or covertly work off-process, because there is an example of an alternative option—that of actively defining an alternative process that better meets the needs of their project. As more and more teams start to customize their process locally, eventually a hybrid process will arise that will be hyped and argued over just as much as Extreme Programming has been.

Summary

- XP is very appealing to programmers but is not suitable for all kinds of projects.
- XP generates few of the deliverables that are expected by other approaches to software development, so handing off an XP application to a traditional maintenance team would be hard.
- XP allows developers to write code that they are proud to show to their teammates.
- "*This is the best project we have ever worked on*" is a really tough act to follow.
- Once a customer is used to being able to steer the project and get a new release every two or three weeks, it would be a real shock to go back to the old ways.

✧ Sooner or later another approach will catch the attention of the software development community and XP will become just another way to develop software.

Part VI

Your Choice

Henry Ford missed an opportunity. He should have sold cans of paint to go with every black car.

Having read this far you know that my conclusion about Extreme Programming is that one size does not fit all. Some projects and organizations are a good fit for Extreme Programming, some are reasonable fits, and some are totally inappropriate places to attempt to use Extreme Programming.

These last two chapters address these questions. We start off by questioning whether Extreme Programming is a good fit for you and your organization, and then proceed to question whether you have an appropriate project for your initial adoption of Extreme Programming. Obviously, there are no hard and fast answers and, even in an organization that cannot effectively apply Extreme Programming, it is often possible to apply many of the lessons of Extreme Programming. Similarly, it may be possible for a team to be successful with XP on projects that are not really suited to XP, even though that same project would not be a suitable candidate for a team new to XP.

Chapter 22

Is XP for You?

Adopting XP is easy. The entire team has to want to use XP and commit to making it work for the whole team.

In the end, it all comes down to how much you really want to use Extreme Programming. Sure, some programmers are clamoring to use it. It will look cool for marketing purposes, and it is always great to add a new acronym to the resume, but do you really and truly want to switch to using Extreme Programming?

This is the key question: Do you really want to adopt XP? After a rational analysis of the various pros and cons, and assuming that XP is suitable for your projects, in the end it comes down to an emotional choice. Are you committed enough to make it happen within your organization? Once you have answered that question for yourself, you have to ask whether your organization is ready for XP.

Is Your Current Approach Broken?

It is very hard to adopt a new process for a marginal gain. If your current approach to software development is working, then it is going to be very hard to justify adopting Extreme Programming. Sure there are claims made for massive increases in productivity from adopting Extreme Programming, but it is very easy to be cynical about these and to suggest that the comparison was really being made against teams using an inappropriate or badly managed process. For a good, enthusiastic, well-managed team using an appropriate process, it is hard to imagine that adopting Extreme Programming would give anything more than a marginal improvement in productivity.

- -

On the other hand, a disillusioned team using an inappropriate process is probably an ideal candidate for a different process. It would be hard for the productivity to go any lower and you might easily get an order of magnitude increase in productivity. So if your process is broken and you are facing disaster, sure, go ahead and adopt a new process; otherwise, it is probably better just to fix your current process.

Is Your Organization Ready for XP?

Is your organization willing to be a pioneer? Is it used to making hard choices and ruthlessly prioritizing between different needs and requirements? The XP Planning Game is all about making hard choices about which features are more valuable and scheduling the most valuable features for development first. Indeed, the Planning Game could be thought of as a litmus test for an organization's ability to make decisions and stick by those decisions. Without the ability to make hard choices, there is no chance for XP to succeed. All too many organizations still seem to think that it is possible to negotiate estimates.

Although it may be feasible to change the overall culture of the organization by introducing XP, it is unlikely that an organization with a Death March [Yourdon, 1997] mentality will be very receptive to XP. The Sustainable Pace that XP mandates is a complete opposite to the usual can-do, macho management of many software companies that insist on so-called "stretch targets" to ensure that the developers are not slacking off.

Do Your Developers Want to Use XP?

Although some developers are really excited by the opportunity to try out XP, many are completely put off by some of the practices. Pair Programming, for example, generates some strong reactions in some programmers who would detest the idea of being forced to work with someone else. Many would much prefer to have a quiet private office so that they can work undisturbed or, failing that, sit in their cubicles with music playing through their headphones to drown out external interruptions. Others find that the Continuous Integration practice puts too much pressure on them to check in their work frequently. They much prefer working at a more studied pace, tackling much larger pieces of work.

In addition, systems analysts, designers, and architects who have progressed beyond programming may be resistant to the idea that there are few noncoding roles in XP projects. Sure, some will welcome the opportunity to start programming again, but many will not.

Is Your Customer Ready for XP?

In many organizations it is hard to get much of a time commitment from the project sponsors. In such an environment it is unlikely that the sponsor will be able to commit to an On-site Customer for the duration of the project. Even if they are, it is unlikely that the On-site Customer is sufficiently senior with enough domain knowledge to steer the project effectively.

Make no mistake about it, the On-site Customer role is a really demanding one. The developers may be working at a Sustainable Pace, but it might not seem all that sustainable to the customer. Indeed, if you wanted to be uncharitable you could say that XP is "the revenge of the programmers." It is payback for all the late nights and weekends that the developers put in. Now the programmers are putting unrealistic demands on the customer.

Are Your Projects Suitable for XP?

Is XP appropriate for the majority of your projects? Regardless of how much your developers want to use XP, it is not suitable for all types of projects. If the majority of your projects involve writing life- or safety-critical embedded software, please don't even think about using XP.

If your projects require large teams, then you are not going to be able to use XP. True, some companies have been experimenting with XP teams of 40 people or more, but most have tried only that after gaining XP experience with small teams. Similarly, if your projects typically require one or two people for a month or so, although it might be interesting to experiment with "solo XP," the projects are too small for XP.

But We Can Overcome These Difficulties

Yes, you can. No doubt about it. If you are sufficiently committed to using XP, you will be able to surmount all of these organizational barriers to XP. The question, though, is whether you are committed to the idea of using XP or more committed to the idea of improving your ability to deliver software applications.

Extreme Programming is not the only option out there. A few alternatives were highlighted in Chapter 4. If there are organizational factors that mean that XP is not a suitable option, it will probably be much more effective to choose an approach that has a better fit with your organization.

Applying the Lessons of Extreme Programming

If you absolutely have to start using XP but it is not a good organizational fit, it may be possible to apply some Extreme Programming ideas in your current development process. In a sense, what you can do is apply the lessons of Extreme Programming [McBreen, 2000].

The basic idea is that you do not have to adopt XP to improve your own software development process. It is possible to lift some of the ideas and apply them within any process:

⋄ XP-style Unit Tests are a very big win even if you are not using Test First Development.

⋄ Nominate a coach to keep your team on process and be intolerant of people working off-process.

⋄ Check in code only when all tests pass.

⋄ Remember that tired humans produce lousy software. Working at a Sustainable Pace is probably a good idea.

⋄ If you want to do incremental development you have to embrace incremental requirements capture [`http://www.mcbreen.ab.ca/papers/IncrementalDevelopment.html`].

⋄ Ensure your projects get a good dose of Reality Therapy. [McBreen, 2000]

Do You Really Need to Adopt XP?

Probably not. For myself, I might suggest it as an option if there were no organizational barriers to XP, but even then I would also suggest alternatives. I have also been in organizations where I have made strong recommendations against XP, even though some developers wanted to use it. Yes, they might have been able to make it work, but my test has always been to ask, "Do we want to do this because we want to use XP or because we want to improve the development process?"

As you may have guessed, I am not a proponent of the idea of using *"stealth" XP* to sneak XP past the process guardians in your organization. Doing so is completely against the values that lie at the heart of XP. Stealth XP can hardly be described as exhibiting courage and communication, and is definitely not showing any respect by hoping that everyone else will be too stupid to notice what is really going on.

In the end it comes down to you deciding if XP is suitable for your organization. If it is and you can get the organizational commitment to using XP, then your next move is to find a suitable first XP project. If the organization does not want to commit to using XP, then you will need to find alternative ways to improve your software development process.

Rolling Your Own Process

There is a middle ground between adopting a new process and improving your current process—that of creating your own process. Although this option should not be undertaken lightly, it is always an option, especially if you have experienced, highly motivated developers and project managers.

If you choose to "roll" your own process, make sure that you are building on successful experience. The roots of Extreme Programming go back to before 1990, in that many of the ideas grew out of the way that Kent Beck and Ward Cunningham worked together to develop software. Ward Cunningham's Episodes pattern language [`http://c2.com/ppr/episodes.html`] was a precursor to XP that looks at software development for entrepreneurial organizations in which the ability to evolve the application continually is important. XP has a different focus than the Episodes pattern language, but many of the themes are common.

Someone, somewhere will eventually come up with another approach to software development that supersedes Extreme Programming. The chances are that this new approach will be created to solve some problems that are unique to a single project, and that this unique solution turns out to be applicable to a wide range of projects. The real challenge for teams will be to understand when local adaptation of a process is sufficient and when invention of a whole new process is necessary.

For most purposes, local adaptation is easier and a lot safer than invention. Successful adaptation does, however, require a lot of reflective thinking about what works and what does not work. A team that could do this consistently for five or more years is likely to come up with a locally adapted process that looks nothing like the original the team started with. Few organizations have the stamina to stay the course of gradually adapting and evolving their own process, but if yours does, then "rolling your own" may be an option.

Summary

- Is your organization ready for XP?
- Can you see major benefits for adopting a new process?
- Is your organization used to making hard choices and ruthlessly prioritizing between different needs and requirements?
- Are all of your developers really excited by the opportunity to use XP?
- Are your project sponsors ready for the time commitment that XP involves?
- Although you can overcome the barriers to XP, it is probably not advisable to do so. Extreme Programming is not the only option out there.
- Many of the lessons of XP can be successfully incorporated into other processes.
- Using *stealth XP* to sneak XP past the process guardians in your organization is completely against the values that lie at the heart of XP.
- Someone, somewhere will eventually come up with another approach to software development that supersedes Extreme Programming.
- For most purposes, local adaptation of an existing process is easier and a lot safer than inventing a new process.

Chapter 23

Do You Have a Suitable
First Project?

I wonder what thoughts went through the head of the first bungee jumper.

So, if you have really convinced yourself that you want to do XP, and have commitment and support for XP from your organization, the next question is, have you got a suitable project and suitable team of developers?

One thing that is definitely missing to date from the XP literature is the idea of a suitability filter as described in the DSDM manual. The overall idea is that

> *DSDM is not the panacea to all project ills that developers seem perpetually to be promised. There are classes of system to which the method is most easily applied and these are the areas that an organization, which is less experienced in RAD, should focus on to begin with. . . . I am loathe to say that the method should never be used for a particular sort of application or platform. Whenever this sort of statement is made, someone always turns up shortly afterwards and says, we did it!* [Stapleton, 1997, p. 19]

The XP community has not, to date, been as explicit as DSDM about the types of projects and organizations that are suitable for XP. In part, this probably reflects an underlying theme that XP can probably be adapted for most types of projects. I am convinced, however, that for organizations contemplating their first use of XP, an XP suitability filter would be really useful.

Assessing Projects for Suitability to Extreme Programming

Although the various XP sites have FAQs [`http://www.xprogram-ming.com/xpmag/whatisXP.htm`, `http://www.jera.com/techinfo/xpfaq.html`], none seem to make it easy to answer the question, "Is this project suitable for XP?" To address this, here is a starter set of questions you can use to help you decide if a project is suitable for your first foray into Extreme Programming.

1. **Is there someone who can fulfill the requirements of the On-Site Customer Role?** If you cannot get a senior, knowledgeable person into this role, forget it. True, you might be able to get some systems analysts to act as a surrogate On-site Customer, but you don't want to try this on your first project. You need a senior person who can be a committed part of the team who is going to spend a lot of their time thinking about and steering the project. XP needs very high involvement from the person who is in the On-site Customer role. Think of this question as the ultimate test of organizational commitment to the project and XP. If a senior, knowledgeable person cannot be spared, then the project is not important enough for it to be successful with XP.

2. **Are the requirements flexible?** The On-site Customer cannot really steer if they are reading from a list of prioritized, fully elaborated use cases. The real benefit of Agile methods is that they can be steered so the team is "building the right system rather than what was originally requested." [Stapleton, 1997, p. 21] Without the necessary flexibility, the Planning Game is impossible and the team will not be able to deliver on emergent requirements at the expense of the originally envisioned features. Rather than a written requirements document, you need an On-site Customer with a clear vision of what is wanted.

3. **Does your team have the right mix of experience?** Ideally your team should have a good mix of experienced developers, intermediates, and novices. Yes, after you have experience with XP you might be able to get away with using an unbalanced team, but it would be a mistake on your first XP project.

4. **Is the entire team committed to using XP?** Sorry, but skeptics need not apply. All it takes is one person not really willing to follow the process for your first attempt at XP to end in a dismal failure.

Programmers who refuse to pair, refuse to write tests, or leave code checked out for days at a time are a guaranteed way to spoil the team dynamics. Yes, they might come around in time, but you don't want that type of stress on your first XP project.

5. **Have you got a good coach for the team?** Ideally the coach should have experience working on in XP project, but as a minimum they should have read the books and visited with an XP team and observed how it works. Again, you might get away with less, but that probably isn't the way to bet on an important project when the business is making a serious investment of a senior person's time.

6. **Is the team the right size for an XP project?** Ideally you want a team of six to eight programmers for your first project. The team should be experience heavy; you do not want many novices in the team. Sure, once XP is established and understood in your organization, you can use the XP team as a training ground for novices, but that is not an ideal way to start out.

7. **Is the project the right size and complexity?** Real-time, embedded, and safety-critical applications are not ideal candidates. You need a project that will take a small team somewhere between 6 and 18 months to deliver the desired functionality. The best projects are those in which the On-site Customer can see real benefits from early, partial delivery so that the team can make a production release within two or three months. If you cannot make a useful release within three months, the project is probably too complex for your first attempt at XP.

8. **Can you colocate the entire team in a suitable room?** Yes, later you can experiment with distributed XP if you want to, but initially you need the right facilities. This means one room set up for the exclusive use of the team and is conducive to pair programming.

9. **Does your development environment support rapid feedback?** You want to be able to write a test and then run it to show the failure within a few tens of seconds. Smalltalk, Ruby, and Python are ideal because you can run the test without even having to stub out the called methods. Sure the test will fail, but you are not slowed down by having to stub out methods, save files, compile, and link before running the test. Some Java environments, like

Visual Age for Java, also support the very rapid feedback needed for Test First Development, but even with these the feedback cycle is slower than with the more dynamic languages. You also need to be able to run the entire unit test suite within a few minutes because longer test cycles make Continuous Integration slow and impractical.

10. **Are your delivery timescales flexible?** As you take your first steps into XP, the project will run slower and less predictably than subsequent XP projects. If there is an absolute fixed date by which a certain amount of functionality must be delivered, then it would be risky to adopt any new process. Eventually, all XP teams settle down to a predictable, sustained, and sustainable pace, but initially you should expect the pace to be very unpredictable and uneven.

Answering no to any of these ten questions should cause you to think long and hard before deciding to make this project your first XP project. Yes, an experienced XP team would probably not find any of these to be showstoppers individually, but that is not the point. What you need to do for your first XP project is to set it up for success. If you cannot meet these minimum conditions, I would strongly question whether the project is suitable for Extreme Programming.

Preparing Your XP Team

Once you have determined that you have a suitable project, you also need to make sure that you have a suitable, prepared team. You need to make sure that your XP team has the necessary support while it becomes familiar with the technologies that enable Extreme Programming: the unit testing frameworks, the source code control tools, and the automated build tools. Until the entire team understands how to use these tools as an integrated part of the development environment, your team is not ready to start the first development iteration.

Yes, the Coach should be able to show the team members how to use these tools, but your planning still needs to allow time for the team to become familiar with the tools. If the team is not given sufficient familiarization time, it will be all too easy for the team to revert to previous, non-XP practices, which could easily spell doom for the project.

Summary

- ❖ Is there someone who can fulfill the requirements of the On-Site Customer Role?
- ❖ Are the requirements flexible?
- ❖ Does your team have the right mix of experience?
- ❖ Is the entire team committed to using XP?
- ❖ Have you got a good coach for the team?
- ❖ Is the team the right size for an XP project?
- ❖ Is the project the right size and complexity?
- ❖ Can you colocate the entire team in a suitable room?
- ❖ Does your development environment support rapid feedback?
- ❖ Are your delivery timescales flexible?
- ❖ Do not forget to allow plenty of time for the team to become familiar with XP and the tools that support XP.

Epilogue

"I come to bury Caesar, not to praise him."
—*William Shakespeare, 1599;* Julius Caesar, act 3 scene 2

This has been a very interesting book to write. When I first heard about Extreme Programming I was very excited because I actually enjoy programming. Over time, my questioning of Extreme Programming has led me on a journey that is practically the opposite of Anthony's eulogy for Julius Caesar as told by Shakespeare.

At the end of Anthony's eulogy, the mob is on Caesar's side and is lusting for revenge on the conspirators who killed Julius Caesar. In my case, I started off very enthusiastic and, over time, became much less so because of the very narrow applicability of Extreme Programming. Sure, XP teams have managed to do great things, but suitable projects are few and far between. I have yet to work on a project that was really suitable for XP and I suspect that few other developers have.

. Yes, if you can meet the preconditions, Extreme Programming can be very successful, but so would practically every other approach to software development as well. True, Extreme Programming is nearly unique in insisting that organizations create the right conditions for the project to be successful, but the reality for most projects is that they must be carried out in suboptimal circumstances. Common problems are things like facilities that make it impossible to colocate the entire team, slow decision making, and users being inaccessible. Any and all of these factors create circumstances under which Extreme Programming as originally defined cannot be used.

One way around this difficulty is obviously to attempt to bend XP to fit the circumstances. "Distributed" XP is one example of how a team can attempt XP without being colocated. Other teams have tried XP without an On-site Customer, without Pair programming, and even without organizational support. In the end, though, I think all of these attempts miss the point of Extreme Programming.

For me, it all comes back to the statement that Ron Jeffries made in Oslo that the "Entire team agrees this is the best project they've ever been on." The whole purpose of using Extreme Programming is playing to win. Rather than accepting suboptimal compromises, find a project that enables you to do Extreme Programming the way that it is meant to be done. After all, *Software development is meant to be fun. If it isn't, the process is wrong.*

Bibliography

And now for some light reading . . .

[Auer, 2002] Auer, Ken, and Roy Miller. *Extreme Programming Applied*. Boston: Addison-Wesley, 2002.

[Baetjer, 1998] Baetjer, Howard. *Software As Capital*. Los Alamitos: IEEE Computer Society, 1998.

[Beck, 2000] Beck, Kent. *Extreme Programming Explained*. Boston: Addison-Wesley, 2000.

[Beck and Cunningham] http://c2.com/doc/oopsla98/paper.html.

[Beck and Fowler, 2001]. Beck, Kent, and Martin Fowler. *Planning Extreme Programming*. Boston: Addison-Wesley, 2001.

[Boehm, 2002] Boehm, Barry. "Get Ready for Agile Methods, With Care." *IEEE Computer* 2002; 35(1):64–69.

[Boehm, 1981] Boehm, Barry, et al. *Software Engineering Economics*. Englewood Cliffs: Prentice Hall, 1981.

[Brooks, 1995] Brooks, Frederick. *The Mythical Man Month*. Reading: Addison-Wesley, 1995.

[Coad, 1999] Coad, Peter, Eric leFebvre, and Jeff DeLuca. *Java Modeling in Color with UML*. 1999.

[Cockburn, 1997] Cockburn, Alistair. *Surviving Object Oriented Projects*. Reading: Addison-Wesley, 1997.

[Cockburn, 2001] Cockburn, Alistair. *Writing Effective Use Cases*. Boston: Addison-Wesley, 2001.

[Cockburn, 2000] http://c2.com/cgi/wiki?PrettyAdventuresome Programming.

[Cockburn, 2002] Cockburn, Alistair. *Agile Software Development*. Boston: Addison-Wesley, 2002.

[Cockburn and Williams, 2001] Cockburn, A., and L. Williams. "The Costs and Benefits of Pair Programming." In Succi, G., and M. Marchesi, *Extreme Programming Examined*. Boston: Addsion-Wesley, 2001.

[Constantine, 1995] Constantine, Larry. *Constantine on Peopleware*. Englewood Cliffs: Prentice Hall, 1995.

[Coplien, 1995] Coplien, J. and D. Schmidt eds. *Pattern Languages of Program Design*. Reading: Addison-Wesley, 1995.

[Crocker, 2001] http://www.xp2001.org/xp2001/conference/papers/Chapter15-Crocker.pdf.

[Cunningham, 2001] http://c2.com/cgi/wiki?SystemofNames.

[DeGrace, 1990] DeGrace, Peter, and Leslie Stahl. *Wicked Problems, Righteous Solutions*. Yourdon Press, 1990.

[DeMarco, 2001] DeMarco, Tom. *Slack*. New York: Broadway Books, 2001.

[Fowler, 1997] http://www.martinfowler.com/articles/thud.html.

[Fowler, 1999] Fowler, Martin. *Refactoring*. Reading: Addison-Wesley, 1999.

[Fulton, 2002] Fulton, Hal. *The Ruby Way*. Indianapolis: SAMS, 2002.

[Gabriel, 2001] http://www.dreamsongs.com/LessonsFromNothing.html.

[Gamma, 1995] Gamma et al. *Design Patterns*. Reading: Addison-Wesley, 1995.

[Gause, 1989] Gause, Donald, and Gerald Weinberg. *Exploring Requirements: Quality Before Design*. New York: Dorset House, 1989.

[Gilb 1988] Gilb, Tom. *Principles of Software Engineering Management*. Reading: Addison-Wesley, 1988.

[Green, 1997] Available at http://www.mindprod.com/umain.html.

[Highsmith, 2000] Highsmith, James A. *Adaptive Software Development*. New York: Dorset House, 2000.

[Humphrey, 2001] Humphrey, Watts S. "So Why Don't They Practice What We Preach?" Available at http://www.sei.cmu.edu/publications/articles/practice-preach/practice-preach.html.

- -

[Hunt, 2000] Hunt, Andy, and Dave Thomas. *The Pragmatic Programmer*. Boston: Addison-Wesley, 2000.

[Jackson, 1995] Jackson, Michael. *Software Requirements and Specifications*. Reading: Addison-Wesley, 1995.

[Jeffries, 2001] Jeffries, Ron, Ann Anderson, and Chet Hendrickson. *Extreme Programming Installed*. Boston: Addison-Wesley, 2001.

[Jeffries and Hendrickson, 1998] Jeffries, Ron, and Chet Hendrickson. *Chrysler C3 Payroll*. Smalltable Solutions, 1988.

[Jones, 1994] Jones, Capers. *Assessment and Control of Software Risks*. Upper Saddle River: Prentice Hall, 1994.

[Kaner, 2002] Kaner, Cem, James Bach, and Bret Pettichord. *Lessons Learned In Software Testing*. New York: Wiley, 2002.

[Kidder] Kidder, Tracy. *The Soul of a New Machine*. London: Penguin Books, 1982.

[Leuf, 2001] Leuf, Bo, and Ward Cunningham. *The Wiki Way*. Boston: Addison-Wesley, 2001.

[Marick, 1998] Marick, Brian. "Testing Foundations." Available at `http://www.testing.com/writings/automate.pdf`, 1998

[McBreen, 2002] McBreen, Pete. *Software Craftsmanship*. Boston: Addison-Wesley, 2002.

[McBreen, 2000] `http://www.computer.org/Proceedings/tools/0774/07740421.pdf`.

[McConnell, 1996] McConnell, Steve. *Rapid Development*. Redmond, WA: Microsoft Press, 1996.

[Morales, 2002] Morales, Alexandra Weber. "Going to Extremes." Available at `http://sdmagazine.com/documents/sdm0201a/0201a.htm`.

[Nonaka, 1995] Nonaka, Ikujiro, and Hirotak Takeuchi. *The Knowledge Creating Company*. Oxford: Oxford University Press, 1995.

[Pavlicek, 2000] Pavlicek, Russell. *Embracing Insanity: Open Source Software Development*. Indianapolis: SAMS, 2000.

[Raymond, 1999] Raymond, Eric. *The Cathedral and the Bazaar*. Sebastopol: O'Reilly, 1999.

[Reeves, 1992] Reeves, Jack. "What Is Software Design?" 1992. Available at `http://www.bleading-edge.com/Publications/C++Journal/Cpjour2.htm`.

[Rollings, 1999] Rollings, Andrew, and Dave Morris. *Game Architecture and Design*. Scottsdale: Coriolis Technology Press, 1999.

[Schwaber, 2002] Schwaber, Ken, and Mike Beedle. *Agile Software Development with SCRUM*. Upper Saddle River: Prentice Hall, 2002.

[Spolsky, 2000] Spolsky, Joel. "Things You Should Never Do, Part I." Available at `http://www.joelonsoftware.com/stories/storyReader$47`, 2000.

[Stapleton, 1997] Stapleton, Jennifer. *Dynamic Systems Development Method*. Reading: Addison-Wesley, 1997.

[Vlissides, 1996] Vlissides, J., J. Coplien, and N. Kerth, eds. *Pattern Languages of Program Design 2*. Reading: Addison-Wesley, 1996.

[Yourdon, 1996] Yourdon, Edward. *Rise and Resurrection of the American Programmer*. Upper Saddle River: Prentice Hall, 1996.

[Yourdon, 1997] Yourdon, Edward. *Death March*. Upper Saddle River: Prentice Hall, 1997.

Index

Beck, Kent, *continued*
  on simple design, 63–64
  on team size, 113
  on XP testing, 111
Beedle, Mike, 38, 114, 168
"Best practices" concept, 8
BigDesignUpFront, 98, 154
Boehm, Barry, 19, 20, 31, 61, 77, 119,
    126, 127
Broken software development processes,
    9, 10, 12
Brooks, Frederick, 43, 49
Bugs, 107, 142
  applications full of, 134
  costs of fixing, 122, 124, 127
Bug triage, 108
Build tools, automated, 182
Burnout, 79
  and "Death March," 83

C

C++, 16, 111
Canceled projects, 26
Capers Jones, 133
Capture/playback testing tools, 109
CASE tools, 42, 43, 102
Cathedral-style projects, 36
Change, 26
  costs of, 7, 12, 119
  reevaluating costs of, 7–8
  and reinterpretation of experience, 47
  in requirements, 133
  and requirements traceability, 134–135
  speed of, 136
Change control and emergence, 93
Chief Programmer concept, in
    Feature-Driven Development, 43
Coach, role of, 86–87, 130, 131, 132,
    181, 183
Cockburn, Alistair, 13, 38, 48, 50, 60,
    89, 130
Code, 3, 19
  Extreme Programming and focus
    on, 16
  hard-to-test, 108–109
  intention-revealing, 139
  obfuscated, 67
  reviews, 84

"Code rot," 114
"Code smells," 64, 156
Coding Standards, 71, 75, 86, 162
Collective Code Ownership, 65, 67, 71
Colocated teams, 39, 183, 186
Commitment, to XP, 180–181, 183
Communication, 85, 86, 155
Comparative studies, of Extreme
    Programming, 6
Complexity
  managing, 99–100, 103
  and project size, 181, 183
  system, 143
Computing power, cheapness of, 111
Continuous Integration, 64, 65–66, 69,
    86, 131
  developers preferences and, 174
  and rapid feedback, 182
Continuous reflection, 88–89
Conversations, requirements made
    into, 135
Coplien, Jim, 90
Copy-and-paste programming, 155
Cost-of-change curve, 48
Costs
  and ad hoc projects, 33
  of fixing bugs, 122, 127
  of fixing design errors, 122–123
  of fixing errors of understanding,
    124–125
  and methodologies, 21
  minimizing for user community,
    126, 127
  of releases, 125–126
  of requirements changes, 120–122, 127
  of switching to different approaches, 51
  and waterfall projects, 33
Cost-to-fix, 119
Courage, 85, 86
Cowboy coder, and game development, 34
"Cowboy coding" practices, 4
CRC cards, 100
Cross-training, 90, 91
Crystal, 14, 40–41
Culture
  and approaches chosen, 52
  understanding, 48
Cunningham, Ward, 15, 38

and cost of requirements change, 121
as demanding role, 136
empowered, 148
and errors of understanding, 122
and Good-Enough Software, 108
knowledge of, and changing
    requirements, 135
and maintenance documentation,
    141, 143
persons to fulfill role of, 180, 183
and project size, 181
and requirements changes, 133
significance of, 80–81
and System Metaphor, 65
and testing, 106
transitioning away from Extreme
    Programming, 167–168, 169
working without, 186
XP-readiness and, 175
Open questions, 60–61, 74–75, 81–82,
    89–90
Open Source, 14
Open Source projects
    Cathedral/Bazaar, 36–37
    factors considered important by,
        36–38
    and Ruby community, 37–38
Optimizing approach, 52
Oral documentation, 139–144
Oral tradition, 140
Organizational behavior, and success with
    planning game, 60, 61, 62
Organizational values and culture, and
    approaches chosen, 52
Organizations, XP-readiness for, 174, 178
Outsourcing, 143
Overdose effect, 129–130, 131
Overtime, 82, 83, 84

P
"Painting yourself into a corner," 16, 22
"Pair debugging," 84
Pair Programming, 5, 80, 86, 99, 147
    and code quality/maintainability, 162
    controversy around, 82, 84
    and Small Releases, 130
    strong reactions to, 174
    working without, 186

Partial compliance, 130–131, 132
Partial knowledge, 28, 45
    and Adaptive Software Development, 40
    and Agile methods, 39
    and Crystal, 41
    and Dynamic Systems Development
        Method, 42
    environments, 27
    and Feature-Driven Development, 43
    and Pragmatic Programming, 44
    and Scrum, 45
Partial requirements, 136
PERT (Program Evaluation Review
    Technique) charts, 61
"Plan-driven" approaches, 19, 20
Planning, incremental development,
    57–62
Planning Game, 58–59, 60, 86, 130,
    168, 174
    and flexibility, 180
    organizational behavior and success
        in, 62
    separation of roles and responsibilities
        in, 62
Planning phase, in Extreme
    Programming, 56
Playing to win, 145–149, 186
    and experienced teams, 147
    and novice teams, 147
    and risk management, 146
Practitioners, and anecdotal evidence, 7
Pragmatic Programmer, The (Hunt),
    43, 156
Pragmatic Programming, 43–44
Predictable deliveries, and game
    development projects, 34
Pretty Adventuresome Programming, 89,
    130, 132
    XP distinguished from, 154
"Principle of Least Surprise," and Ruby
    community, 38
*Principles of Software Engineering
    Management* (Gilb), 57
Problem decomposition, and complexity
    management, 99
Process
    limits, 115–116
    signs of broken, 9, 12

Process, *continued*
   as situational, 8
   understanding, 48
Productionizing phase, in Extreme
    Programming, 56
Productivity, 10, 30
   and decline in enjoyment, 131
   with small teams, 113, 116
   team, 87
   XP, and step up in, 149
Program Evaluation Review Technique
    charts. *See* PERT charts
Programmers, 97, 98, 100, 109, 146
   and active pairing, 80
   appeal of Extreme Programming to, 3
   elevating status of, 159
   knowledge about testing by, 105–106
   maintenance, 142, 144
   retraining, 167
   XP's strong appeal to, 162, 166
Programming, 3, 30, 120
   copy-and-paste, 155
   literate, 139
   and waterfall projects, 32
Project progress, and acceptance test
    scores, 109, 112
Project risks
   Extreme Programming and addressing
    of, 25–26
   as symptoms, 26–28
Projects
   comparing, 51
   complexity and size of, 181, 183
   locking into XP practices, 166
   long-running, 114
   suitability of, for XP, 175
Project sponsors, and XP-readiness,
    175, 178
Project teams, 10
Python, 101, 111, 181

Q
Quality assurance, 45, 106

R
Rapid feedback, support for, 181–182
Raymond, Eric, 36
Reeves, Jack, 95, 96, 99, 155

Refactoring, 4, 64–65, 66, 68, 69, 71,
    76, 86, 99, 130, 131, 156, 167
   and Acceptance Tests, 73
   and code quality/maintainability, 162
   and Collective Code Ownership, 65
   and design errors, 123
   and Test First Development, 72, 73
Refactoring (Fowler), 49
Regression test suites, 76
Release dates, 59
Release Plan, 58, 59, 130
Releases, 126, 136
   cost of, 125–126
   and Planning Game, 58
   and retraining On-site Customer,
    167–168
   testing, 106
Requirements
   changes in, 133–134
   costs in changes in, 120–122, 127
   emergent, 135–136
   flexible, 183
   freezing, 133, 134, 137, 168
   specifications, 96
   testable, 75, 77, 109
Requirements creep, 133
Requirements traceability, and change,
    134–135
Respect
   as core value in XP, 85, 91
   and Sustainable Pace, 86
Return on investment, 51, 62
Reverse engineering tools, 166
Rigorous methodologies, 21
Risk(s), 28
   examples of, 25–26
   and fears, 26
   management of, 29, 45, 146
   mitigation of, 15, 58
   as symptoms, 26–28
Rolling your own process, 177–178
Ruby, 37, 75, 101, 111
   projects, 101
   and rapid feedback, 181
Ruby community, issues important to,
    37–38
Runtime errors, and Smalltalk
    programs, 18

S

Safety critical projects, 52
Scalability of processes, 93
Scaling, and process limits, 115
Schedule slips, 25, 26, 28
    and Acceptance Tests, 73
    and Big-Design-Up-Front approach, 98
    planning practices and minimizing
        of, 57
    and Simple Design, 64
Schwaber, Ken, 39
Scope creep, 133, 136
Scrum, 14, 44–45, 114, 127
    hybrids based on, 168
    issues of importance to, 44–45
Selection problem, and Bazaar style, 36
Setting the dials on ten, 129, 132
Shipping schedules/dates, 62, 148, 149
Short-cycle, incremental development
        practices, 69
Short delivery cycles, 127, 160
Short iterations, 57
Shrink-wrapped application software, 30
Simple Design, 63–64, 66, 69, 70, 72,
        73, 86, 99, 100, 117, 131, 140
    and Acceptance Tests, 73
    and code quality/maintainability, 162
    and Collective Code Ownership, 65
    and Continuous Integration, 66
    and design errors, 123
    and Do The Simplest Thing That
        Could Possibly Work, 156
    OnceAndOnlyOnce as part of, 155
    and refactoring, 64
    and YAGNI, 154
Simplicity, 85, 86
Situational processes, 12
Slack (DeMarco), 83
Slow-moving environments, and freezing
        requirements, 134, 137
"Smallest, most valuable set of stories,"
        delivering, 57, 62
Small Releases, 57–58, 59, 60, 61, 86, 126
    and cost of fixing design errors, 123
    and fixing errors, 125
    and Pair Programming, 130
Smalltalk, 15, 16, 18, 25, 111
    community, 100

    programmers, 101
    and rapid feedback, 181
Small teams, 113, 116
    and complexity management, 99, 100
    working with, 116
Software
    design, 95–96
    maintenance and evolution of,
        49–50, 53
"Software: The New Realities"
        (DeMarco), 21n.1
Software architecture, and Unified
        Process, 35
Software Craftsmanship (McBreen), 8
Software development, 3, 4–5, 151
    alternative approaches to, 131
    changing assumptions about, 10
    competing ways of, 13
    and complexity management, 99
    and cost of change, 7
    current approach to, and adopting XP,
        . 173–174
    as design activity, 96–99
    economics of, 61
    forms of, 30
    and risk, 25
    situational processes in, 8
    and transitioning away from Extreme
        Programming, 165
    and viability with small teams, 116
Software development community, and
        software engineering community, 162
Software development methodology, 18
Software development processes,
        understanding, 10
Software development teams, and playing
        to win, 145–146
Software engineering approaches, 14
    ad hoc projects, 33–34
    game development, 34
    overlap between XP approach and, 102
    traditional waterfall projects, 31–33
    Unified Process projects, 34–36
Software engineering community
    disconnect between XP community
        and, 159
    and software development
        community, 162

Software Engineering Economics (Boehm), 7, 31, 119
Software engineering projects, factors considered important by, 30–35
Soul of a New Machine, The (Kidder), 33
Source code, 97, 144
    control tools, 182
    as design, 95–103, 155
    as primary documentation, 139
Specialization, 32, 90, 97
    Speculate-Collaborate-Learn cycle, and Adaptive Software Development, 40
Spiral Development, 61
Spolsky, Joel, 49
Staff turnover, 26, 79
    and "Death March," 83
    and long hours, 80
    reducing, 80
    and System Metaphor, 65
    and Test First Development, 72–73
Stealth XP, 177, 178
Stories, and cost of requirements change, 121
Stretch targets, 60–61, 174
Structured programming, 30, 102
Suitability filter, 179
Suitable projects, for Extreme Programming, 179–183
Sustainable Pace, 80, 81, 82, 83, 84, 86, 174, 175
Sustained and sustainable delivery, 28
Sutherland, Jeff, 39
System complexity, and handoffs, 143, 144
System design documents, 96
System Metaphor, 65, 73, 86, 99, 100, 140
    and application architecture, 69
    and code quality/maintainability, 162
    criticism of, 68
System of Names pattern, 65
Systems analysts, 136, 137, 166, 175

T

Tacit knowledge, 19, 20, 22
Tailorable methodologies, 21
Takeuchi, Hirotak, 19

Teams
    building, 91
    and coaches, 86–87
    colocating, 181, 183
    commitment to XP, 183
    continuous reflection by, 88
    and freezing requirements, 134
    improving social dynamics of, 79
    mood of, 131
    of novices, 147, 149
    right mix of experience in, 180, 183
    size of, 113, 181
    studying, 5
Testable requirements, 75, 77, 109
Testers, 98, 109, 136
Test First Design, 5, 66
Test First Development, 72–73, 74, 76, 86, 108, 110, 111–112, 120, 131, 167
    and Acceptance Tests, 73
    and failing tests, 144
    and fixing errors of understanding, 124
    and maintenance teams, 142, 143
    and rapid feedback, 182
Testing, 30, 31, 45, 71, 74, 96, 97, 102, 120
    as preventive mechanism, 124
    specifications, 96, 98
    and waterfall projects, 32
Testing community, role of, in projects, 110
Thomas, Dave, 39
"Timeboxed" development, 41
Torvalds, Linus, 160
Traceability, and Unified Process, 35
Traditional software development, and large teams, 113
Traditional software engineering approach
    applying XP within, 114
    and handoffs, 140, 141
    and Moore's Law, 110–111
    and requirements changes, 137
    requirements viewed by, 133
Traditional software engineering teams, and documentation reviews, 139
Traditional waterfall projects, 31–33

Also Available from Addison-Wesley

Software Craftsmanship

The New Imperative

By Pete McBreen

0-201-73386-2
©2002
Paperback
208 Pages

As the demand for software has exploded, the software engineering establishment has attempted to adapt to the changing times with short training programs that teach the syntax of coding languages. But writing code is no longer the hard part of development; the hard part is figuring out what to write. This kind of know-how demands a skilled craftsman—not someone who only knows how to pass a certification course.

Software Craftsmanship presents an alternative—a craft model that focuses on the people involved in commercial software development. This book illustrates why it is imperative to turn from the technology-for-its-own-sake model to one that is grounded in delivering value to customers. **Pete McBreen** presents a method to nurture mastery in the programmer, develop creative collaboration in small developer teams, and enhance communications with the customer. The end result is skilled developers who can create, extend, and enhance robust applications.